The End of Captivity?

The End of
CAPTIVITY?

A Primate's Reflections on Zoos,
Conservation, and Christian Ethics

Tripp York

Foreword by Laura Hobgood-Oster

CASCADE *Books* • Eugene, Oregon

THE END OF CAPTIVITY?
A Primate's Reflections on Zoos, Conservation, and Christian Ethics

Cascade Books
An Imprint of Wipf and Stock Publishers
199 W. 8th Ave., Suite 3
Eugene, OR 97401

www.wipfandstock.com

ISBN 13: 978-1-62564-753-5

Cataloging-in-Publication data:

York, Tripp

The end of captivity? : a primate's reflections on zoos, conservation, and Christian ethics / Tripp York ; foreword by Laura Hobgood-Oster.

xxii + 136 p. ; 23 cm. —Includes bibliographical references.

ISBN 13: 978-1-62564-753-5

1. Animal rights—Religious aspects—Christianity. 2. Animals—Religious aspects—Christianity. 3. Human-animal relationships. 4. Animal welfare. I. Hobgood-Oster, Laura, 1964–. II. Title.

BT746 .Y67 2015

Manufactured in the U.S.A.

Unless otherwise indicated, scripture quotations are from the New Revised Standard Version Bible, copyright 1989, Division of Christian Education of the National Council of the Churches of Christ in the United States of America. Used by permission. All rights reserved.

"How an Animal Advocate Ended Up in a Zoo" is a revised and extended version of the previously published chapter "Should We Intervene in Nature? A Brief and Timid Defense of Zoological Gardens," in *A Faith Encompassing All Creation* (Eugene, OR: Cascade, 2014).

"Can the Wolf Lie Down with the Lamb without Killing It?" is a revised and extended version of the previously published chapter "Can the Wolf Lie Down with the Lamb without Killing It? Confronting the Not-So-Practical Politics of the Peaceable Kingdom," in *A Faith Embracing All Creatures* (Eugene, OR: Cascade, 2012).

For Duncan, Ginger, Mango, and Kramer: captives no more.

The obsession with putting ourselves at the center of everything is the bane not only of theologians but also of zoologists.

—YANN MARTEL, *LIFE OF PI*

Contents

Foreword

A s a child growing up in the shadow of Washington DC, the National Zoo (part of the Smithsonian Institution) was a place we frequently visited either on school field trips or with family and friends. I remember loving it because anything and everything having to do with animals excited me. I also remember feeling that there was something deeply wrong, but I couldn't name what exactly seemed so tragic about it. I just know that there was a moment when a fabulous silverback gorilla looked me in the eyes through the glass that kept us apart and tears started to flow from me uncontrollably. He didn't want to be there and he seemed to be asking for release. But there was nowhere else for him to go.

In this lovely, thoughtfully written book, Tripp York tackles the question of the zoo—and of captive animals in general—within a complex theological framework. Why do humans have animals in captivity? What is the purpose of this practice? Is it valid, humane, worthwhile—and for whom? Do we need to end captivity? If so, then what becomes of the animals who have no habitat left outside of zoos? The possibilities suggested here open up significant space for dialogue and reconsideration.

Because York spent hundreds of hours working directly with animals in captivity, his voice carries an authority that is filled with actual experience. Shoveling elephant poop (which, while it can be repulsive, York declares necessary and good) for two years gives one a new perspective on the life of animals in captivity. He also engaged with keepers at a variety of zoos and delved into the history of these institutions. Zoos have obviously not been a stagnant reality. Both a remnant and current embodiment of colonialism, they do come with a fraught history—and their present status is also laden. Some are much better than others in terms of their ability to keep animals in environments that provide the possibility of a good life in captivity. Some serve different purposes than others.

These experiences allow the author to enter into conversations with both a much-needed critical voice and one that is empathetic to those who do spend hours working in zoos and advocating for their necessity and even for the benefits they offer to both humans and some other animals. Speaking with proponents and opponents of zoos also provides a wide-ranging sense of how adamant humans can be about these places of animal confinement. York does not defend zoos outright, but he does not condemn them completely either; rather, he complicates the easy answers sometimes offered about whether they are always good or always bad. Different zoos are, well, *different*. Even for those opponents who think all zoos should be opened and animals set free (think of the movie *Seven Monkeys*), the questions and ideas posed here open up space for understanding.

This book gives a call for consistency, thoughtfulness, and significant engagement when thinking about and advocating for captive animals (yes, even those who are confined in the process of becoming food—the numbers are staggering). And it calls for a new vision of a truly eschatological, embodied Christianity. It is at this turn, when York offers insights into why animals and captivity matter theologically, that the center of his story comes to light. There emerges from his words an elegant, though not naïve, grace in the gift of relationships with other animals. We humans need to learn to approach them with the "as if" of potential friendship and mutual joy rather than approach them as if they do not matter at all. York invokes Steve Irwin and Jane Goodall—both inspirational figures who, while they certainly have not been theological witnesses, have been amazing animal witnesses.

In some of his most recent work, science writer Carl Zimmer discusses the evolutionary benefits of animal friendships. Both within species and across species lines, friendship makes individuals stronger. And while often the stories of a tortoise and a hippo or a dog and an orangutan as best buddies bring smiles, the scientific evidence is mounting that connections, alliances do matter. On the deepest level, York is posing many of the same questions and challenging those who claim Christianity as their faith system to realize that such friendships are integral to this religious tradition. The entire creation groans for redemption, and we have a responsibility to move in the direction of the peaceable kingdom, as complicated as that move might be.

As York asks in various ways throughout the book, is zoo life better than no life at all? Indeed, that is the overarching question. Life in captivity might be the only life left for some animals—and that, likely, is due to human greed. This thought-provoking book gives every person who has advocated for or against zoos, and even those who have never really thought about the depth of that question, a new sense of the pragmatic and theological significance of the end(s) of captivity.

Laura Hobgood-Oster
Southwestern University

Acknowledgments

I am grateful to the various zoos, sanctuaries, conservation and science centers that took time to field questions, schedule interviews, and allow me to visit their institutions and wildlife parks. Their openness and hospitality are greatly appreciated. I was often surprised by the willingness of so many people to take me in and answer my sometimes muddled attempts at coherent questions. Many thanks, in particular, to social behavior and wildlife conflict expert Bruce Schulte, who set me up with the elephant staff at Grassmere Zoo and the Louisville Zoo. All of the folks at both zoos were incredibly generous with their time. Many thanks to Rainhill Equine Center and the Duke Lemur Center. Although I was unable to include your interviews, I still appreciate the time you made for me. What I learned about blind horses and critically endangered lemurs is not as impressive as what I learned about the people willing to care for them.

I owe a very special debt of gratitude to Mindy Stinner at the Conservators Center. Mindy is a smart, caring, hard-working, and wickedly funny person who, despite her insane schedule, always found more than enough time for my persistent badgering. She also made it possible for me to spend an afternoon with a baby caracal and a very rowdy Geoffroy's cat. I hope, for everyone's sake (especially Naja's), that Renato has calmed down a bit. Though, of course, not too much.

I also owe an immense debt of gratitude to the gracious folks at the Virginia Zoo. First of all, allow me to state that though I was a volunteer at the Virginia Zoo for close to three years, serving as both a keeper aide and a writer, any and all opinions, unless otherwise stated, are mine and are not representative of the Virginia Zoo. With that being said, many thanks to Executive Director Greg Bockheim and Assistant Director Roger Sweeney. Despite your busy schedules, both of you always made time for me. I appreciate it. Many thanks to the two keepers I worked with the most, Dennis McNamara and Jason Strohkorb. Thanks for the excellent training and your toleration of my incessant questioning, and for allowing me inside a world of incredible animals. I hope I helped you guys more than I hindered you. Thanks to Wyn and Aubry Hall for access to the zoo library and, more importantly, to the squirrel monkeys. I hope it saddens you when you think about how you left me here in Virginia.

I need to give a very special thanks to all of the keepers, vet staff, and folks in administration, including Jill Tarrant, Adrienne Esson, Leah Rooker, Martha Hamilton, Craig Pelke, Win Danielson, Patti Bernhardt, Jim Lotz, Lee Strickland, Linda Brandt, Denise Luckey, Brooke Akright, Brooke Wilson, Meg Puckett, Rosanne Runyeon, Caryn Wachenfield, Allyson Zahm, Shaun Stauffer, and Jennifer Long. All of you were consistently helpful, open, and just all-around awesome. I never imagined I would find myself in the position of being defecated on by a squirrel monkey, urinated on by a gibbon, and, best of all, scratching the ears of a white rhino.

Finally, I owe a very special debt of gratitude to Ryan Andrew Newsome who provided the name for the book, and to those who read earlier drafts and offered excellent comments, criticisms, and editorial notes. Many thanks to Jacob Martin, whose editing skills turned this into a readable book, and to both Morgan Stroyeck and Melanie Kampen, who went well beyond the call of duty. Apparently, I now owe Morgan a surfboard. That's fair. Melanie, I'll figure something out for you if you ever decide to leave Canada. To the loveliest biologist I know, Carly Anne York: Thank you for allowing me to tiptoe in your domain. I apologize for not always heeding your suggestions. I'm an obstinate primate that way, which, I'm sure, you already know.

Introduction: The Papal Pachyderm

Look at Behemoth, which I made just as I made you.

—JOB 40:15

In 1514, King Manuel I of Portugal presented Pope Leo X with what would become the pontiff's most treasured gift: a white elephant named Hanno. We don't know if Hanno was actually an albino, but we do know from the writings and artwork of Hanno's time that she was an Asian elephant of very light skin. In India, Hanno's original home, white elephants were often treated with special favor. Rare as they were, these elephants were provided with a number of servants to accommodate the special status afforded them. Such honored status made Hanno an obvious, albeit unusual, gift for the pope. King Manuel's present was an astounding success. The pope was not only impressed with the elephant, he was smitten with her. Leo's love for Hanno, and his feeling that such love was reciprocal, would become so strong that he once said he was "almost tempted to put faith in the assertion of the idolaters who pretend that a certain affinity exists between these animals and mankind [*sic*]."[1]

It is interesting to note that the pope thought a "certain affinity" between humans and other animals was a form of heresy—or, in his words, idolatrous. We are well aware that there is more than a certain affinity that exists between animals. There are gorillas who love kittens, orangutans who love dogs, hippos who love turtles, and humans who love them all. Such an

1. Bedini, *Pope's Elephant*, 57.

affinity makes sense—they are, after all, our biological and covenantal kin. The pope certainly felt such an affinity, as is evidenced by his reaction to Hanno's sickness. When Hanno ceased eating, Pope Leo called in the greatest physicians of his time and told them to spare neither effort nor expense in saving her. Though no expense was spared, no one in sixteenth-century Rome was qualified to diagnose an elephant. The doctors treated Hanno as they might treat a human and gave her an enema. This was no ordinary enema, however; it was an enema befitting a papal elephant. It was an enema laced in gold. Unfortunately, the royal enema did not relieve Hanno of her constipation; it killed her. The pope was devastated.

Upon her death, Leo immediately demanded an appropriate memorialization of Hanno. Poets wrote poems, lyricists wrote lyrics, and an artist no less immortal than Raphael was commissioned to create a large mural to be placed in the piazza of St. Peter's basilica. Imagine visiting the most sacred site in Christendom only to discover, at its entrance, a fresco of a white Asian elephant. It is borderline absurd, yet in the most interesting of ways. Here, in the heart of Christendom, was a masterfully painted reminder that creation includes life other than human life. Just as God created Behemoth (which may or may not refer to the elephant), God created humans (Job 40:15). As confused as we may be when it comes to thinking about animals, if nothing else, the one thing we do know is that we share a common creator. It only makes sense, therefore, that the holy sites of Christianity would include depictions of other life forms. Without them, we would be giving a poor account of creation. In the Christian narrative, redemption and communion with God is for all life, not just human life. While it may strike some of us as absurd that our holy sites include artistic renderings of other animals, it is this kind of absurdity that underwrites the story of Christianity. The Christian narrative claims that the peaceable kingdom is an animal kingdom. While humans may operate with a different purpose than other animals, the chief purpose of all flesh is the worship of God. That Christians have often depicted images where all flesh worship God is not unusual. If anything, they are simply following John's account in Rev 5:13: "Then I heard every creature in heaven and on earth and under the earth and in the sea, and all that is in them, singing, 'To the one seated on the throne and to the Lamb be blessing and honor and glory and might forever and ever!'"

The notion that other animals glorify God is nothing new to the Christian tradition, though it is rather scandalous. After all, it fuels some of the antipathy many opponents of Christianity have toward the "irrational" nature of Christianity, while also demanding that Christians take a more serious look at the purpose of other creatures. In terms of the latter, this may require Christians to both think and act differently toward other animals. It is not enough to simply believe, think, or imagine that the peaceable kingdom is an animal kingdom; we must embody such a claim. The only danger/scandal here is that we could end up producing more people who look like St. Francis. That is, in the eyes of those who do not envision such a kingdom, we could end up looking a bit foolish.

Yet, it is in such foolishness that we find the resources necessary to imagine what it would mean to embody our claims about the peaceable kingdom. In particular, what does it mean to claim that the peaceable kingdom is an animal kingdom, and what might that look like in the now? For the purpose of this book, I'm particularly interested in the role zoos, sanctuaries, and conservation centers play in terms of how their practices do or do not contribute to our collective imaginations about the importance of the rest of the animal kingdom. Specifically, I want to address how our captivation with other animals has often led to their captivity and what such captivity says about us. For example, while it may be the case that Hanno should be symbolically present in paintings, it is not clear that she should be physically present in Rome. Though the peaceable kingdom includes the animal and plant kingdoms, there are, statistically, few animals and plants that can thrive in all parts of the world. Animals originate in certain areas and, except for a small number of species, remain in that area. That we find an elephant in Rome, or, for that matter, in the United States, should strike us as rather strange. Not only do I live three miles away from two African elephants, I spent two years working in their stalls and yard. While it was incredible to be in the presence of these animals, I continually found myself asking, "How, and why, did these African elephants end up in Norfolk, Virginia?"

How these two elephants ended up in southeastern Virginia is a long and complicated story. For some folks, it may be a story of tragedy, while for others it may be a story of hope. It's probably a little bit of both. It all depends on the vantage point. At this juncture, I'm more interested in how any exotic animals end up in captivity. Of course, the reasons why we keep animals in captivity vary greatly. We could never accurately generalize about animal captivity. Some folks keep exotic animals in captivity as an exercise in power and for the display of status. Others may keep exotic animals in captivity for the purpose of scientific curiosity and research (which may or may not be to the benefit of a particular animal or species). Some animals are maintained in captivity for the sake of those individual animals and for the conservation of their species, while other people hold animals captive for nothing more than their own voyeuristic entertainment. To be sure, there are many different reasons why we house animals in human-built edifices—some of which are ethically disturbing while others are morally uplifting. The history of menageries, zoos, circuses, sanctuaries, wildlife centers, bio-research facilities, as well as the ongoing domestication of wild animals, is incredibly convoluted and defies any easy reductionism. It is difficult to reduce the existence of the housing (or caging) of animals to any one aspect. There seem to be many factors at work, all stemming from various motivations, some of which are good and some of which are bad.

What I want to examine is what it means to occupy this planet with so many other animals knowing that there is no perfectly consistent manner by which we can respond to all other animals. I want to simply ask a few questions and explore a few areas that will complexify a bit of what it is we think we are saying when we talk about the good of other animals. In particular, I will address how we talk about the good of other animals in light of a stark impossibility: their freedom from us. That is, all of us in this reality called the animal kingdom are related, intertwined, and dependent upon one another (granted, ants and bees may not need us in the same way we need them). There can be no hands-off approach, as such an idea is ecologically, philosophically, and, for some people, theologically naïve. Such thinking is ill-informed as to how our very existence is intimately tied to the millions of life forms that constitute our shared planet. We are intertwined with animals we do and do not know. They provide us with food, comfort, mental and physical health, as well as perform specific roles that enable the kind of biological diversity necessary for humans to thrive. Surely, both the atheist and the theist can agree that such a reality is a gift— a precarious gift, to be sure, as it is one that is constantly under threat from our own carelessness with that which sustains life.

In this book, I will explore a number of questions about other-than-human animals; by doing so I hope to say something not only about who we think *they* are but also who we think *we* are. I believe this is a significant question rarely examined. It is important because the manner by which we name the role and purpose of other animals reveals who it is we think we are and how we understand our place and purpose. That is, what do elephants, tigers, and horses performing in circuses say about how we see the world? What does the reality of zoological parks say about the people who create, support, decry, protest, and patronize them? Are sanctuaries preferable to zoos? How important is wildlife conservation for the good of the earth? What does "who" we put on our plate say about how we either do or do not understand the purpose of creation? Do faith commitments serve to work for or against the just treatment of other animals? What constitutes the just treatment of other animals, and what sort of criteria should be employed when discussing that which we consider just or unjust? These are just a few questions I will attempt to work through as I think about the purpose of keeping animals captive.

The *End* of Captivity?

There is a dual sense in which I am employing the word *end*. First, I am referring to it in the sense of finality. In Christian theology, this is referred to as eschatology: the doctrine of the last things. Second, and perhaps more importantly for this book, I am using the term in the Greek sense of *telos* or purpose. That is, to what end are we created? To what end do we serve? For my purposes, I'm not referring to the possible end of captivity in the sense that animals, including us, shall be captive no more; rather, I am addressing what purpose, if any, captivity serves. Even when I am talking about the end of captivity, as in the ceasing of it, I am also asking about the end of captivity in terms of its purpose. If eschatology is, ultimately, about the end, then it seems only right to discuss the end to which the end serves.

To put it simply: How does the captive animal serve the purpose of that which she was created to serve? Perhaps it is the case that such captivity thwarts her purpose. Then again, perhaps it doesn't. To think well about this subject, we will have to distinguish between the varying degrees of difference that constitute one form of captivity from another. Not all forms of captivity are equal. It is far too easy to call for the end of captivity as if we know exactly what that means or what that will look like. On a planet with little so-called wild remaining (and no end in sight to our own encroachment), some form of captivity (zoos, sanctuaries, conservatories, reserves, and wildlife parks) seems inevitable. It is for these reasons that we may need to ask if captivity is a suitable situation for those who have nowhere else to go. We may even need to ask if the term *captivity* is an appropriate term for any and all situations. It could be the case that what we refer to as captivity may offer an otherwise unattainable reality—a reality some may alternatively refer to as freedom.

A Primate's Reflections on Zoos, Conservation, and Christian Ethics

Taking a cue from the story of Leo and Hanno, I was inspired to think more about the place of zoos, conservation centers, and sanctuaries in an effort to determine why they exist, how they differ from one another, and how they do or do not function as places of safety for those animals that humans collect. I am not comfortable with the word *collect*, though I understand that some zoo folks refer to their animals as collections. I have been told that such language leads one to imagine that these facilities are to function as living museums. Again, I am not terribly comfortable with such a description, but we will have to see if such a description is fair or at odds with the well-being of the animals collected.

Ultimately, all I offer here are a few modest reflections on the time I spent working in a zoo as well as my time with innumerable folks working in various sanctuaries and wildlife centers. There is no way I can come close to including all of their collective wisdom and, occasionally, antagonism toward one another within these pages. It may be the case that I do a follow-up to this book comprised entirely of interviews and conversations with people who represent such institutions. That is not what I wanted to do with this book—though I did, for the sake of allowing space for other voices, include a few interviews.

If you are reading this and are already antagonistic toward zoos, I ask that you bear with me and remain open to the possibility that not everything about zoos is as you imagine it to be. Likewise, if you are a strong proponent of zoos, I hope that my criticism of them is met with the drive to turn zoos into the kind of biological conservatories they often claim to be. For anyone whose desire is genuinely for animal welfare, we would all be much better off not simply calling for the closings of zoos but calling for zoos to become what they purport to be: places of education and conservation. On this point, I think anti-zoo organizations like Born Free, In Defense of Animals, and People for the Ethical Treatment of Animals can find some common ground with those who have dedicated their lives to the betterment of individual animals who, for whatever reason, ended up in a zoo. This will require folks on all sides of the debate to attempt to put aside ideological differences for the betterment of the animals who find themselves in the middle of the debate. After all, it is not about who is right; it is about creating the kind of space in which all animals can live healthy, flourishing lives.

In the case of Hanno, whether or not she was freer in the wild of India or in the care of one the most powerful humans on earth will depend largely upon your definition of freedom. There are advantages and disadvantages, in both worlds, for Hanno. Certainly she received a kind of attention, lavishness, and care she would otherwise not receive in the wild. Nevertheless, most of us probably cannot help thinking that the advantages of life with her own family clearly outweighed whatever advantages she gained with human keepers. She was deprived of her home, her family, and her own way of life so that she might be a gift, a token, given by one powerful person to another. This does not mean that she was not cared for and loved. Pope Leo was actually ridiculed for caring too much for Hanno. Even after Leo died, people continued to make fun of his love for the white elephant. Some Protestant reformers even used his love for her as evidence of the corruption of the Catholic Church.[2] I would like to think that, whatever faults Leo X had (and, as with all of us, they were legion), his genuine love for Hanno was real. Does such love justify the moving of an elephant from India to Rome? No. The very idea that an elephant can function as a gift from one person to another should strike us as grossly problematic (though why this is less problematic in the case of a dog, gecko, or a cockatiel is not always clear). Five centuries later, however, many of us are a mere short drive away from an elephant. Though the reasons for our proximity to exotic animals are often complicated, what I hope is not complicated is what it means to show care and compassion for those who are so very often at our mercy. It is for their sake, and ours, that we need to think well about what it means to house other species.

2. Bedini, *Pope's Elephant*, 152–53.

1

How an Animal Advocate Ended Up in a Zoo

If zoos are like arks, then rare animals are like passengers on a voyage of the damned.

—Dale Jamieson, *Morality's Progress*

I have heard nearly as much nonsense about zoos as I have about God and religion.

—Yann Martel, *Life of Pi*

Between the years of 2011 and 2013, I became an avid shoveller of elephant and giraffe poop. How it happened remains, to this day, a bit of a mystery to me. During those years, many of my students and colleagues would ask why I was doing it. For me, the answer was in the question. It's not every day you find yourself in a position to clean up after a five-ton animal. How could I not do it? At the same time, I'd long been suspicious of the place, purpose, and role of zoos. In sympathy to Jamieson's quote above, I'm reluctant to jump on board with the idea that zoos are symbolic representations of modern-day Noahic attempts to save animals.

Noah did, after all, release the captive animals. Zoos, on the other hand, have a slightly poorer track record. Granted, one reason for Noah's success is that he actually found space to dock the ship in order to let the animals go. Such abundant space is far more difficult to locate these days. Getting the animals off ship is not necessarily the captain's responsibility.

Prior to my work in the zoo, I visited numerous conservatories and animal sanctuaries in the Southeast. I wanted to learn more about those who rescue animals from bad situations as well as what they thought of those who advocate for captivity or relocation of animals in the name of education and conservation. I'd read so much literature arguing for and against zoos that I thought the best way to learn was to spend time with folks who are on friendly and unfriendly terms with zoos. Ultimately, I decided to meet with various zoo officials in order to find a way to serve behind the scenes in a zoo. After doing so, I contend that this is the best way to actually learn about what it is that zoos do and do not do. Most other forms of knowledge, I have found, are rooted too much in hearsay, rumor, speculation, and untrustworthy internet memes.

My time in the zoo was also, oddly enough, precipitated by a seminar I had recently taught at Western Kentucky University. The course was rather ostentatiously titled "Living Lives That Matter." Given the name of the class, and what it suggests, I was probably the least qualified person on campus to teach it. Regardless, I jumped at the opportunity to teach the course. I was fortunate to have a bright group of students, and together we worked through some big questions: Are some lives more significant than others? What does work have to do with what it means to be human? What does a meaningful life look like? What do religion, love, death, work, politics, family, and friendship have to do with living a life that matters?

As you can well imagine, it was the kind of course that needed to be longer than one semester.

We spent the majority of our time reading as many different authors and relevant books as I could cram into one semester. We examined biographies, essays, novels, short stories, and plays. We read everyone from Homer to Emma Goldman, from Aung San Suu Kyi to Will Eisner. Actually, the main problem with the class was that all we did was read. In retrospect, a little less reading and a little more doing would have been helpful in working through some of the guiding questions.

In my normal attempt to indoctrinate my students on those matters I find important (after all, professors profess), I included a section on wildlife conservation. Initially, this struck a number of my students as quite odd. After all, when it comes to life's big questions, doesn't it make more sense to read Aristotle, Shakespeare, and Simone Weil? Why bother reading Annie Dillard's take on weasels or learning why Clem Coetsee stressed the importance of dehorning rhinos? Indeed, when surrounded by the safe concrete walls of the university (where the only nature students typically encounter is in a sterile biology lab), such readings did seem to be a bit of a stretch.

As we started to examine some of the complex and oftentimes contradictory saints of the wildlife conservation movement, such as Helen Freeman, Dian Fossey, Lawrence Anthony, and Steve Irwin, my students began gravitating toward the vision these conservationists shared. This process was due not to any verbal arguments made by these activists; rather, my students found these people compelling because of the tangibility of their lives. What these conservationists did, what they contributed to the world and how they lived, was so utterly concrete. Whether it was Fossey's fight for the gorillas, Anthony's relationships with elephants, Freeman's unparalleled work with snow leopards, or the eccentric passion that drove Irwin to fall madly in love with crocodiles, my students were moved by their ability to live life passionately—as if it were a gift. Though there was much my students disagreed with in the lives and writings of these individuals, they were all impressed by the fact that they at least lived lives worthy of discussion. That, in and of itself, is an achievement.

Of course, I don't think any of these people lived as they did just to provoke a discussion. I think they did it because of their convictions about the purpose of human existence. In this sense, the way they lived was their best argument for how they viewed the good that is creation. Their lives assumed the kind of purpose that directly said something about what it means not only to be human, but to treat life as a gift and to be a gift to others. Finding such lives worthy of conversation remains, I think, a theological imperative.

We discovered that the witness of folks like Fossey and Anthony required us to reimagine what it means to live well among the millions of other species that several major faith traditions, such as Judaism, Islam, Hinduism, and Christianity, claim are the work of God. We found ourselves wondering why wildlife conservation was such a consistently ignored topic in the field of religious ethics. Take, for instance, Christianity: For a body of people quick to claim that creation is good, we often fail to spend much time living as if creation is good. That is, there seems to be an overwhelming failure, in terms of practice, to embody the claim that creation is good. Our neglect, our abuse, our concentrated destruction of the land, of forests and the countless species that reside in, on, and above the earth, all seem to suggest that we do not actually believe our own claims. And if we don't believe them, why should anyone else believe them?

Tabling such an important question for now, we eventually raised other questions in our seminar: How can we live meaningful lives that are also mindful lives? How can we live lives that are in concert with nature rather than in opposition to it? For those of us who express religious convictions about the way the world was created, how do we live doxologically ordered lives that see the chief end of *all* existence as communion with God? On that score, doesn't the preservation of animals and their habitats become not only an ecological necessity, but a theological necessity as well? Perhaps, as intimated above, such preservation even takes on a missional tone. That is, how can the manner by which we exist on this planet, in conjunction with the millions of other species and countless forms of organic life, not be a part of who we claim to be in light of what Christianity claims about the good of the earth? How could we ever imagine that we could somehow separate our claims about life from how we live life amidst all of these other lives? Those were some of the questions we addressed, and it was those kinds of questions that led me out of the university classroom.

A Shipwrecked Ark

I don't mean to defend zoos. Close them all down if you want (and let us hope that what wildlife remains can survive in what is left of the natural world).

—YANN MARTEL, LIFE OF PI

Fast-forward a year and I'm working through those questions by serving as a Keeper Aide in the Virginia Zoological Park in Norfolk, Virginia. To be fair, my fascination with rhinos, sloths, and squirrel monkeys may have played a significant role in my decision to serve as a Keeper Aide as well, but I've always been interested in, even if suspicious of, how zoos can function, metaphorically and literally, as both an ark and a garden. In their attempts to be both an ark and a garden, zoos have the potential to militate against apathy toward nonhuman life. They have the means to demonstrate, to those who would otherwise never be able to see, the effects of our en-croachment on the rest of the world.

Many people are rightly divided on the subject of zoos. To put it lightly, they have certainly had a tumultuous history. What we know as the modern zoo has its origin in nineteenth-century conceptions and Victorian ideals surrounding nature. In terms of a much longer history, it can be argued that zoological parks originated approximately five thousand years ago.[1] We know that King Shulgia (2094–2047 BCE) of Mesopotamia kept a number of exotic creatures, and that Queen Hatshepsut, of the Eighteenth Dynasty, was responsible for the first recorded animal-collecting expedition (around 1490 BCE).[2] From the ancient Egyptians to Chinese and Roman emperors, the housing of exotics was often practiced for a variety of reasons: respect and awe of nature, religious belief and piety, display of power and wealth, or scientific investigation. The showcasing of animals, for whatever reason, has a long and varied history that, in many ways, culminates in the modern zoological park.

Zoos today, at least the ones accredited by the Association of Zoos and Aquariums (AZA), boast an emphasis on conservation and education. The modern zoo attempts to achieve a number of goals, including the protec-tion of genetic resources (which makes breeding and release programs pos-sible), financially contributing to wildlife conservation and field research, and functioning as a school of public education that teaches its visitors the importance of biodiversity.

What is of particular interest to me is how zoos can serve to function as a good for all animals and how that good can be adjudicated amidst the tension of displaying nonhuman animals for the entertainment of human animals. After all, the large contribution that zoos make to conservation and education would not be possible if no one paid to see the animals. A key tension that many conscientious keepers, curators, and zoo directors have to negotiate is the one between natural habitats and good exhibits. Depending on how you see it, a good exhibit can make for a bad habitat, and a good habitat can make for a bad exhibit.[3] Many animals retreat from

1. Hancocks, *Different Nature*, 6–8.

2. Croke, *Modern Ark*, 129.

3. Much research has actually shown that the more natural the habitat the more in-clined visitors are to view the animals in that habitat, even if they can't see them, in a more positive light. This suggests that it is actually in the best interest of the claims that zoos make about animal welfare and conservation to ensure that a habitat is as natural as possible—even at the expense of making it difficult for humans to see the animals. See,

the presence of humans, so a conscientious zoo will do everything it can to give animals a place to hide from the public eye. Of course, zoo visitors do not pay to see animals in retreat. This becomes a difficult balancing act for zoos. Good zoos show the utmost concern for each individual animal while also being aware that if the animals are not visible to the public then the zoos may not be in business much longer. Indeed, for some people, the fact that many of these animals prefer to retreat from the human eye may be their principal argument *against* zoos.

Such a sentiment, however, reveals a very naïve understanding of zoos, the wild, and how the two do and do not conflict. Many of the animals in zoos were not captured from that supposedly blissful place that humans imagine "the wild" to be. Such a notion betrays a lack of knowledge as to what sort of free spaces do and do not exist, as well as which (and how many) animals can successfully live in them. For example, many people assume that all elephants in zoos were taken as babies from the wild. While there is certainly historical validity to such a claim, many elephants were bred in captivity, and some elephants were actually rescued from what many consider to be the wild. I say "rescued" because the process of culling has been one of the various factors in the placement of elephants in North American zoos. I was recently in a conversation with an animal rights advocate (I live about five blocks from PETA's headquarters, which, in turn, is only a few miles from the zoo) who was trying to convince me that life for African elephants would be better in Africa than in Norfolk. I agreed. No convincing necessary. As a matter of fact, I think most of the people working in zoos would likewise agree, if not for one thing: Where in Africa does a captive-bred or a rescued elephant return? Some of the elephants we have in the United States were not, as discussed above, kidnapped from the wild; rather, some of them were rescued from wildlife parks that, for the sake of a particular ecosystem, practice culling.[4] That is, many wildlife parks, the

---

for instance, Hancocks, *Different Nature*, 111–48, as well as Heini Hediger's now dated, yet still relevant, *Wild Animals in Captivity*. The fact that numerous zoos still neglect to put in place many of Hediger's innovative suggestions from almost half a century ago is certainly a blow to the kind of claims zoos make about their awareness of natural habitats and their importance for animals.

4. Akin to humans, elephants are unique in that they have the ability to drastically alter and destroy their environments in a way unrivaled by most animals. Conservationists in wildlife parks started the process of culling as a means of keeping the numbers of elephants down so that other species, such as the black rhino, would have a chance at survival. Large numbers of elephants have often wreaked havoc on farmlands, creating a volatile conflict between humans and elephants in various areas of South Africa. This,

very space often assumed to be the bastion of complete and unadulterated freedom, practice population control. What many well-intentioned people fail to understand is that Africa is doing what she can to put a fence around herself. Much of what passes for the wild is, in reality, a park with borders. Almost everything is managed. In fact, one of the major problems is that the parks are not managed well enough.[5] Not only are there ongoing issues with poaching (something the AZA fights via the allotment of financial resources), but the basic human-elephant conflict, a conflict rooted in survival, is never-ending. This conflict, along with poaching and the destruction of natural habitats, is, in some areas, decimating the elephant population (while in other areas, the population of elephants may be too high). Such destruction of our earth and its inhabitants means that there is little wild left to which the elephants could return. The occasional zoo visitor who bemoans the supposed plight of captive animals often imagines an Edenic wild existing in Africa, one that just happens to be hospitable to all living creatures and has yet to be encroached upon by humans. Such an idea is groundless. Such land does not exist (or at least there's not enough of it). Even if we could, to stay with the example of elephants, send them back to their original homeland, where would we send them? People just assume that we could round up hundreds of elephants, who have never known anything but captivity, and deposit them in some safe haven in Africa. Whose end would that serve? It certainly would not serve the elephants. In Africa, their populations are tightly managed in parks—which, again, is how, apart from captive-bred elephants, some zoos end up with elephants in the first place. That is to say, some elephants are brought to North America because there is nowhere else for them to go. They might otherwise be killed in the very places, large parks in South Africa, that many zoo opponents falsely imagine to be free from humans.

This discussion of the nonexistence of viable elephant havens is not to suggest that zoos are the institutional messiah of pachyderms. The size and

---

too, led to culling. Culling was banned in South Africa in 1995, yet this ban was reversed about thirteen years later with the concomitant spike in their elephant population. Due to the work of folks like Lawrence Anthony, as well as many animal rights agencies, most parks attempt to employ birth control, translocation, and range manipulation as forms of management prior to considering culling. Either way you look at, it is human intervention; intervention of some sort seems unavoidable.

5. Ronald Tobias argues that, despite the large tracts of managed land in Africa, 80 percent of an elephant's range is unprotected by government agencies. They simply lack the financial resources to protect the species, leading to arguments for tighter herd populations on less land. See, for instance, Tobias, *Behemoth*, 422.

space of habitats that zoos offer an elephant is abysmal compared to what scientific studies suggest an elephant requires. According to a 2006 U.S. Fish & Wildlife Service study, an elephant needs a living space of approximately eighty square miles. Even if that number is inflated, it is safe to say that elephants in Kenya's Tsavo National Park receive only a pittance—about 1.5 square miles of range, on average. This is fifty times less than the space suggested by the U.S. Fish and Wildlife Service. If that sounds appalling to you, consider this: the elephants in Tsavo National Park still receive almost *two thousand times* the space the average elephant in a North American zoo receives.[6] In terms of life span, only 2 percent of captive elephants live beyond the age of fifty. These same elephants live half as long as many elephants in various national parks in Africa. Ronald Tobias points out that even elephants working in Burmese labor camps live more than two decades longer than an elephant in captivity in North America.[7] Based on those numbers, it should be clear why anyone would be reluctant to argue for the superiority of zoo life over life in protected and managed parks. I am simply suggesting that zoo life may be better than no life at all.[8] I am also suggesting that, while it is obvious that certain animals are, theoretically, better off outside of captivity, one cannot make generalized assumptions about the kind of ecological politics that force animals into captivity. Just because, for example, the lemurs of Madagascar have far more space to roam than in The Lemur Center at Duke University does not make The Lemur Center at Duke a bad place. The Lemur Center at Duke is one of the few institutions in the world doing anything to stave off lemur extinction. They are doing

6. These numbers are from Ronald Tobias's seminal history of elephants in the United States, *Behemoth*, 426.

7. Tobias, *Behemoth*, 433–34. There are numerous reasons for these worrisome statistics, and it may be the case that these numbers are misleading. For example, one method of gaining these numbers includes only animals that are dead and does not factor in living elephants. Based on that sort of methodological analysis, if an elephant in a zoo has a stillborn baby, or if an elephant dies in her first year of life, then, of course, the average life span of captive elephants will be perversely low. There are many different methods for estimating life expectancy and, with each method, the results will differ widely. One of the most detailed reports outlining the difficulties with obtaining credible statistics comes from Robert Weise and Kevin Willis's thorough and technical report, "Calculation of Longevity and Life Expectancy in Captive Elephants."

8. While this may or may not be the case for certain megafauna, many species can thrive in captivity. This is not an endorsement of captivity. I just cannot pretend to occupy the kind of lofty position by which I could suggest, for other animals, that death is better than captivity—especially when I have witnessed how life is for some captive animals.

incredible work for the good of the individual animals in their care and for the species as a whole. Therefore, it is a good place despite the inevitable space limitations, because its efforts are for preservation. So, while zoos can never come close to offering the kind of space an elephant in the wild or a managed park inhabits, this fault based on limited resources does not make a zoological park a bad place. It certainly does not make it an ideal place, but it does not make it a bad place. It is our never-ending encroachment on the world of animals that continues to lead to their captivity. This encroachment requires thoughtful human beings to come up with alternatives to culling, extinction, habitat decimation, and the loss of entire ecosystems. It is for these reasons that zoos are starting to become an alternative to what is beginning to look like a no-win situation.

Such no-win situations for many animals have led some animal advocacy groups to argue for a hands-off approach to the wild. Yet, anyone who demands that we cease all projects of intervention is, quite possibly, living on another planet.[9] Nonintervention is impossible. We intervene constantly—even when we are unaware of it. Whether it is the farmlands that feed us while disrupting the homes of groundhogs; the clear-cutting of forests that spells disaster and extinction for countless animals; the building of roads, tunnels, and bridges that displace innumerable animals; the inadvertent burying of gopher tortoises under construction lots in Florida; or the poaching of rhinos and elephants throughout Africa, human beings are constantly intervening in the lives of animals. There is no hands-off approach. The question is not *whether* we are going to intervene; the question is *how* we are going to intervene.

This is where zoos, along with other conservation-based entities, can be a good thing. Note that I say they *can* be a good thing. I am not blindly suggesting that zoos are exemplary practitioners of animal welfare and conservation, only that they have the potential and, from a practical standpoint, the resources to become the kinds of places where good work is accomplished. Indeed, many of them have been doing this for years. I have

9. When zoos in both San Diego and Tampa rescued a number of elephants from execution in Swaziland, many animal rights advocates argued it would be better for the elephants to be systematically executed than to live a life of captivity. Without even responding to the hubris one must embody to declare another animal is better riddled with bullets than living in a zoo, I can wholeheartedly say that, in visiting some of these elephants and seeing their habitats, their daily enrichment, their diets, and their relationships with zoo staff, such "advocates" are wrong. For more information on this topic, see French, *Zoo Story*, 1–21.

conversed with zoo directors, curators, keepers, wildlife conservationists, and biologists of all stripes, and the one thing they almost all agree on is that there is little hope for many currently endangered species surviving in some space free from human intervention. This is not pessimism. This is simply an informed lack of confidence in light of what we are doing to the land. The primary enemy of animal advocates, therefore, should not be those who house animals; the primary enemy of animal advocates should be the loss of our natural habitats. Much of it is gone, and what is not protected and managed is quickly disappearing. Due to the loss of natural habitats, zoos, along with sanctuaries and a number of conservation-based agencies (many of which collaborate with zoos), are becoming one of the few remaining options available for preserving animal species. Until the wholesale destruction of ecosystems comes to a halt, I am not sure there is much hope for many of our currently endangered species remaining in their native environments. Therefore, in terms of the sordid history of zoos, the question is not so much what they were doing last century or even a decade ago, but what are they doing now and what can they do in the future? Can they become the kinds of places that practice hospitality to animals in need? Can they offer something that is quickly becoming absent in this world? That is, can they become a good replacement home for animals who are losing their natural homes?

A Gateway?

Zoos, from the most awful to the world's best, expose a perpetual dichotomy, which is the reverence that humans hold for nature while simultaneously seeking to dominate it and smother its wildness. They reveal both the best and the worst of human nature.

—DAVID HANCOCKS, *A DIFFERENT NATURE*

The above questions are in a constant state of negotiation and I certainly do not have the answers. In the next chapter, I will reflect a bit more on these questions while asking more questions regarding the various roles zoos perform. Zoos have little problem providing reasons for their ongoing existence, but do they actually deliver on their claims? Zoos must move beyond their role of simply offering up a few captive-bred tigers and pandas as evidence of wildlife conservation. Saving a few endangered species through breeding programs, while certainly no small matter, may not be enough if an organization is going to truly own its claims of conservation and education. Zoos must, to quote zoo architect and critic David Hancocks, "become gateways to the wild, metaphorically and practically."[10] To become a gateway may require that the AZA enforce a proposal made to the organization almost thirty years ago. The proposal was that each accredited zoo, in order to retain its accreditation, would be required to adopt at least one habitat, threatened space, or species. The zoo would then fund, via the support of the public (ensuring a community effort), various academic studies of that habitat or species in an attempt to save it. Fortunately, this is already occurring in a number of zoos. What is now necessary is for zoos to become that gateway, perhaps even a true ark, via the recognition of the interrelated nature of all life. Given that zoos have an incredible reach in terms of those who visit them (all ages and economic spectrums), they have the capacity to alter our way of seeing the world. Perhaps if their focus shifted to how ecosystems work, not just the popular animals who dwell in those ecosystems, they could, in turn, provide the public with the resources it needs to understand what is at stake in wildlife conservation. In becoming conservation parks that support research, conservation, and animal well-being, zoos have the potential to grow into the kind of garden that is more than just a poor imitation of the real thing.

Fortunately, many contemporary zoologists are practicing a new direction based on scientifically motivated models of conservation. While zoos certainly do exist for entertainment, their primary purposes, they claim, are education, conservation, and the protection of certain species (ironically) from us. It would seem that, just as Noah built an ark to protect animals from God's punishment, we now build arks in order to protect animals from *human* punishment. Of course, this notion of an ark, as suggested earlier, is a bit of a romanticized notion—if not entirely untruthful. For the most part, zoos, by necessity, tend to ignore the vast majority of endangered animals. Instead, they focus on those animals they imagine the public most wants to see. I do not necessarily fault zoos for this practice. Zoos, like any other institution, are constrained by the limits of time, space, and financial resources. Plus, if the father of sociobiology and one of our most important conservationists, E. O. Wilson, is correct when he claims that we are losing three species every hour, then it is beyond any one entity

10. Hancocks, *Different Nature,* 150.

to be a genuine ark.[11] When the entire planet is in danger, where does one possibly float a ship? We know that nearly all of our large cats are endangered, as are wild horses, sea turtles, antelopes, rhinoceros, gorillas, countless species of birds and amphibians, and many of those animals killed or displaced by deforestation.[12] These instances are not natural forms of extinction; they are human-induced forms of extinction. The sheer number of vanishing animals alone forces any institution, whether it is a zoo or a conservatory, to be more careful about the claims they make. We are not, however, let off the proverbial hook by the recognition that such institutions cannot live up to their own claims. That's far too easy a move for the omnipresent armchair activist. At least zoos are doing something. Oftentimes they are doing far more than what anti-zoo pundits care to discover. Many zoos, in fact, financially contribute directly to field research, while other zoos team up with conservation agencies in an effort to save species, in their natural habitats, precisely so those species do not end up in zoos. Zoos have been responsible for rescuing numerous species from extinction; creating sustainable reintroduction programs; giving millions of dollars to scientific research; and supporting, annually, thousands of scientific and conservation-based research projects, all in an effort to embody the goal of many of the world's very first zoos: to be a garden of scientific inquiry.[13]

Pulling Weeds

The wolf shall live with the lamb, the leopard shall lie down with the kid, the calf and the lion and fatling together, and a little child shall lead them.

—ISAIAH 11:6

To create such a garden, a garden where life abounds, is not just the aim of those who see our natural habitats quickly slipping away; it should be a primary concern for those who claim the story of Christianity. After all, the

11. For a compelling account of why Christians should have much in common with the efforts of conservationists, see Wilson's *Creation*.

12. Here are just a few books that provide an extensive account of the animals and habitats we have recently lost, are now losing, or will undoubtedly lose in the near future: Wilson, *The Future of Life*; Mackay, *The Atlas of Endangered Species*; Sartore, *Rare*; Hoage, *Animal Extinctions*; Corwin, *100 Heartbeats*; and Goodall, *Hope for Animals and Their World*.

13. Norton et al., *Ethics on the Ark*, 253–71.

hope of such a garden, metaphorically reminiscent of Eden, is to embolden our imaginations so that we can faithfully embody the very claims we make about the good that is creation. Just as the prophet Isaiah depicts a compelling image of the original peace restored (11:6–9), these gardens have the potential to offer a glimpse of Isaiah's forthcoming world. In making such a claim I am certainly not trying to idealize zoo culture or to attribute to them an eschatological mindfulness of which they may or may not be aware. I am only suggesting that, placing the many convoluted issues surrounding zoos aside, they are symbolic of our fallen estrangement from, and our eschatological connection to, the rest of creation. As with the lives of our eccentric ecological saints, zoos remind us that, despite our culture's incessant need to spiritualize the material, creation really does matter. Though zoos are part of a history of dominance and control over nature as opposed to co-existence and a willingness to work with nature, they still remind us that all of life is a gift. Such a gift can be respected, enjoyed, and even, in some cases, touched. It is also a gift that can be—and often is—abused, ignored, and neglected.

So, I guess part of the reason I spent two years shoveling poop at the zoo is simply because zoos (and poop) exist. I became involved at the zoo because I wanted to learn something about the plight of other animals on our planet. I wanted to learn, firsthand, how and why so many of these magnificent creatures ended up in my neighborhood. I also wanted to learn whether I should be supporting facilities, like zoos, that hold animals captive. I quickly discovered that there is much to support and much to protest. That's what makes their existence such a difficult thing to quantify. Zoos, like the humans that create, support, and protest them, are a mixed bag. It is only after spending so much time in a zoo that you really learn what is done well, what is done poorly, and what can and cannot be done at all. If nothing else, zoos certainly have incredible potential to become the gardens and gateways they often claim to be.

In this chapter, I simply intended to explain how I came to work in a zoo and how that has allowed me a glimpse into their very complicated nature. One thing I have definitely learned is that I am wary of anyone who offers either blanket condemnations or wholehearted praise of zoos. Either account is reductionistic and can only be made by those who are unaware of all the facts. Proponents and opponents of zoos have much ammunition to use against one another. Such a battle, however, does little to help the animals caught in the middle. The concern is simple: Why do we keep animals captive, and does their captivity behoove the animals or the species to which they belong?

In the next chapter, I will follow some of the ideas presented in this chapter and see if we cannot come to a clearer or perhaps more complex understanding of the nature of zoological parks. I do not pretend to offer any authoritative or final word on zoos. I also will not argue as to why their presence should or should not be supported by those with or without theological leanings. I only want to take a closer look at their claims and why so many of us are either attracted or repulsed by them. I think that both our attraction and our repulsion may stem from the fact that zoos, as with sanctuaries and conservation centers, have the ability to become—and in some ways already are—a symbol of humanity's attempt to save what we have tried to destroy. They offer a glimpse of a partially opened gateway to other worlds and to other nations. They remind us of what we have and how easily it could all be lost. In that respect, they are a collection of living photographs reminding us of what we are losing. They are gardens with weeds, shipwrecked arks, and mountains where wolves live with sheep.[14]

14. Many thanks to Melanie Kampen for reminding me of the importance of weeds. I speak of them here in more of a metaphorical than a literal sense, which may or may not be any more favorable to weeds.

INTERLUDE: "Scatet totus orbis"

Shit is a more onerous theological problem than is evil. Since God gave man freedom, we can, if need be, accept the idea that He is not responsible for man's crimes. The responsibility for shit, however, rests entirely with Him, the creator of man.

—MILAN KUNDERA, THE UNBEARABLE LIGHTNESS OF BEING

In partial agreement with Kundera (certainly not his gender-exclusive language), I'm not terribly fond of poop. I'm not convinced it's a very good argument against the existence of God, but it's safe to say that I, too, find fecal matter repulsive. Nevertheless, prior to my move from the Keeper Aide program to occasional writer for the zoo, I spent many weekend hours shoveling the poop of elephants, giraffes, bongos, ostriches, Egyptian crowned cranes, African ground hornbills, gazelles, porcupines, owl monkeys, callimicos, and numerous reptiles and amphibians. In terms of the latter, I guess I wouldn't call it shoveling per se—more like taking a spoon and scooping it. In some cases, a really, really big spoon. Reticulated pythons can produce some serious crap.

The repellant nature of fecal matter is biological. The typical human aversion to feces probably resides in an instinctual need to distance ourselves from certain forms of bacteria that could be deleterious to our health. Perhaps this is part of the reason why we (and not other animals) find it to be so offensive. It's foul. Malodorous. Stinky and messy.

If I had to rank animal excrement in terms of its offensiveness, at least based on my own personal experience, I'd award first place to that of the otter. Worst poop ever. How a creature so cute could excrete something so wrong is a mystery to me.

Elephant poop is actually quite manageable, as it's so large and compact. I didn't mind cleaning up after elephants. You do, however, have to pick the right size shovel or it will wreak havoc on your back. It's sizeable, and there's just so much of it. Elephants eat and poop all day long. There's never a shortage of those round, multiple-pound, hay-laced mudballs.

The feces of ostriches and Egyptian crown cranes is just a disaster. Forget picking it up. You just have to hose it.

Giraffe dung has forever altered my once insatiable desire for chocolate malt balls. I used to love them. Now, I'll never look at them the same way.

Certain monkeys will examine their poop with the hope of finding a rummaging insect to eat. They only throw it after they've checked it for potential protein. Waste not, want not.

Speaking of monkeys, I've been shat on by a squirrel monkey and peed on by a gibbon. Granted, gibbons are not monkeys. They're lesser apes. Just don't tell them that.

Rhino babies, along with many other species, practice coprophagia— which is code for eating feces. In particular, they will eat their mother's dung. Apparently, they require the bacteria for building a healthy stomach capable of digesting food. I've never witnessed this practice, as the only rhino I've ever been around is in his forties. He has gracefully eased into sexual retirement and is a much, much chiller dude because of it.

Why am I talking so much about poop? To counter Mundera, poop serves many purposes and is a requirement for the well-being of pretty much every ecosystem on the planet. Dung, like sex, makes the world go round. It accumulates on land and on the bottom of the sea floor, and is colonized, in some form or another, for the benefit of that particular ecosystem. Poop is necessary. Poop is good.

The way in which many other animals understand their excrement differs radically from the human experience. We seem to be, as a whole, far more bothered by excrement than most other species. I guess that's part of the reason I find so interesting anyone willing to clean up the waste of other animals. It takes special kinds of people to commit their lives to cleaning up after others. Animal caregivers in zoos, sanctuaries, and wildlife centers devote their lives—regardless of the politics behind the animals' being there, or *whether* the animals should be there—to feeding, caring for, and cleaning up after them. Regardless of where it is done, animal care is messy, smelly, and often monotonous work. Shit is a constant reminder of the material nature of our existence. It defies the temptation to both spiritual-ize and romanticize nature. It reminds us that, regardless of how cute that baby giraffe, elephant, or red panda may be, they are about to shit all over everything. And they're not going to clean it up.

Of course, that's one of the prices we pay for having animals in captiv-ity. In the wild, that excrement would serve a whole host of other purposes. In captivity, it simply has to be cleaned up day after day after day. It's not glorious work, and as I stated above, it requires a certain kind of person to commit her life to such repulsive work. This is one of the reasons why, as critical as I am of zoos (and you should be too), I have little time for people who make grand, sweeping statements about zoos—referring to them as prisons maintained by evil wardens. I hear and read such statements often. Those people do not know the people I know. While there are folks who can make any profession look bad, the majority of keepers and caregivers I have met would do anything for the individual animals under their care. No one loves those particular animals more than they do. I have also found that many people quick to pronounce judgment on the existence of zoos and wildlife centers do so from the comfort of their safe, clean, and fairly pre-dictable middle-class lives. They cast their judgment from a vantage point of great distance. They're far removed from the animals, the people, and all the messiness involved in the politics of zoological parks, wildlife conserva-tion, breeding and release programs, field and scientific research, adoption and rescue missions, veterinary care, cooperation with universities and conservation agencies, and all of the other countless efforts undertaken to slow the tide of species extinction. This distance is quite characteristic of the kind of activist whose only activism is critique. Such folks often remind me of a lovely quote from the rather feces-obsessed theologian Martin Lu-ther who once wrote, "Scatet totus orbis": the entire world defecates.

Some more than others.

2

Neither Eden nor Alcatraz

The following two chapters will not delve into any theological issues related to animal captivity. Instead, I am going to say a bit more about zoos and conservatories in order to set up a conversation as to why such institutions may or may not be of theological importance. I believe what we will discover, as intimated in the first chapter, is that zoological parks and conservation centers are neither prisons nor salvific arks. They may be something altogether different, and it is this difference that is worthy of theological reflection.

Animal Care and the Politics of Eating Old Jim

Zoos are institutions established for human pleasure. . . . Zoos represent the power of human beings to command the presence of living creatures which would normally absent themselves from human gaze.

—BOB MULLAN AND GARRY MARVIN, *ZOO CULTURE*

Between the years of 1866 and 1891, Woodward's Gardens was a fixture on the West Coast. It was San Francisco's first amusement park, zoo, aquarium, art gallery, and museum rolled into one. Woodward's Gardens was a place where people were not only entertained but also educated, primarily about the natural world. It was, for its time, a remarkable achievement. It was re-markable not simply because of everything it featured (from roller-skating rinks to hand-feeding sessions with seals), but for its innovative treatment of caged animals. Many animals, such as deer and ostriches, roamed the grounds freely, while other animals, though certainly confined, were pro-vided the kind of space that made the average zoo of its day look like some of our worst prisons. Indeed, one of the most innovative practices of the superintendent of the zoo at Woodward's Gardens, Louis Ohnimus, was his emphasis on keeping the animals as mentally healthy as possible. While it has taken ethologists and zoologists almost an additional century to dis-cover that the mental well-being of an animal actually matters, Ohnimus understood quite well that the inner health of an animal directly impacts her physical health. Due to his understanding of animals, he was able to produce some rather interesting results. Whereas many zoos of his era had a difficult time keeping animals alive for more than a few years, Ohnimus's emphasis on natural exhibits, enrichment, and concern for the mental well-being of the animals led to their living, on average, five times longer than animals in other zoos.[1] We can only infer that due to his relatively revo-lutionary focus, the animals at Woodward's Gardens, by and large, lived better lives than most other zoo animals.

What would eventually lead to the death of almost all of Woodward's animals was not captivity; it was their impending release. As park visitation began to wane, a campaign against the gardens was led by a minister who claimed that the noises made by the animals were disrupting his Sunday morning services.[2] This, coupled with waning attendance, led to Wood-ward's being shut down, and the authorities ordered that all the animals be killed. One local butcher decided to cash in on the misfortune of these animals and killed one of Woodward's most famous bears, Old Jim. He then served Old Jim as a delicacy to his patrons. What a peculiar, if not consistent, end for a once-beloved attraction. It is a consistent end in the sense that any time we humans view an animal as little more than a com-modity for our enjoyment, we should not be surprised by our ability to make use of that animal in whatever ways benefit us. The fact that Old Jim became food—for the very people who once were awed by his presence—

1. Hancocks, *Different Nature,* 61–62. Certainly, Ohnimus was a product of his time. The argument is not, therefore, that he was the epitome of a perfect caregiver. He sim-ply seemed to figure out, years before many others, the connection between mental and physical health in captive species.

2. Ibid., 61.

should not be terribly surprising. Horrifying, perhaps, but not surprising. If nothing else, the butchering of Old Jim is just a reflection of how confused we often are when it comes to the place, role, and purpose of other animals.

In reflecting back on Woodward's Gardens and seeing what was once a popular attraction now close to being erased from our collective memory (there's now a restaurant there by the same name), a host of questions are raised. How do education and entertainment function in zoological gardens today? What role do zoos play in terms of science, conservation, and animal well-being? Is there any such thing as a healthy and happy animal in captivity? More importantly, what does the presence of zoos say about us? What do zoos say about the people who create them, work in them, and visit them, and what do they say about the people, like the minister mentioned above, who wish, for whatever reason, to shut them down?

To Love or to Loathe?

We should have the honesty to recognize that zoos are for us rather than for the animals.

—DALE JAMIESON, *MORALITY'S PROGRESS*

According to the Association of Zoos and Aquariums (AZA), zoos bring in an average annual attendance of 175 million visitors. That's more than the annual attendance of the NBA, MLB, and NFL combined.[3] Even though there is no zoological equivalent of ESPN running the same show twenty-four hours a day, zoos are a bigger attraction than all of these professional sports put together. What is it about zoos that is so appealing to us? What is it about them that attracts our gaze, and what does our attraction to them say about us?

I asked the assistant director of the Virginia Zoo, Roger Sweeney, this question, and he suggests that much of the appeal of zoos rests in the kind of individual learning experience a person gains from her visit:

> If you look at it from the average visitor perspective, it's about experience and what they expect to get out of that experience. You would think sporting events would be hard to beat. Entire cities revolve around certain sporting experiences, which is a certain type of bonding experience. It's a tribal experience revolving

3. See http://www.aza.org/visitor-demographics/.

around a battle that binds people together. I think the experience
of coming to a zoo is that, typically, you would like to think it is a
green space. It's more peaceful, it's more tranquil, more reflective,
and, hopefully, more educational. I think a huge part of the visitor
experience survey is that people talk about the experience of being
able to share this experience with children for the first time. Zoos
are more about individual experiences, as opposed to the bonding
experience of a sporting event.[4]

I believe that, in many ways, what Sweeney means by individual experiences is wrapped up in how everyone comes away from the zoo with radically different experiences. While some people come away disappointed
that their favorite animal is not visible, others are highly enamored with
the two young male tigers playing in the pool. Some people spend more
time reading the posted literature on each animal than they do looking at
the animals themselves, while other people never even bother to look at the
educational material. Some folks sit for hours—taking photos, attempting
to understand what the orangutans and gibbons are thinking—while others
are interested only in watching a northern pine snake consume a mouse.
Some people leave zoos thinking that zoos are like prisons, keeping animals
against their will from living fully realized lives in the wild, while others
walk away inspired to become wildlife conservationists.

Coming from a background that includes participation in a number of animal rights organizations, I've been exposed to my fair share of
"zoos are everything that is wrong and evil in this world" rhetoric. As with
many grand, sweeping claims (which most often influence the impression-
able—like me), I've discovered firsthand how convoluted is the subject of
zoos. As much as I wanted to find black-and-white answers, such answers
consistently eluded me. Perhaps that's because zoological parks are, as suggested in Yann Martel's *Life of Pi*, much like religion. Martel's protagonist
Pi argues that people tend to maintain certain illusions about zoos and
religion.[5] While these illusions often revolve around certain conceptions of
freedom, people also maintain assumptions about what it is about zoos and
religion that attracts people. Religion has the potential to bring out the best
and worst in human nature—so do zoos. Indeed, it seems that many jobs
that require contact with animals tend to attract the best and the worst kind

4. This was part of a conversation between Roger Sweeney and me that was, initially,
intended to serve as an interview for this book.

5. Martel, *Life of Pi*, 15–19.

of people. We are inundated by countless stories of animal abuse in zoos, circuses, sanctuaries, shelters, pet stores, veterinary clinics, various wildlife service agencies, farms, and in our own homes. That other species of animals often suffer abuse by humans is surely a matter worthy of discussion. What is it about other animals that elicit such wide-ranging responses from so many people? I imagine it has much to do with how we, subconsciously or not, define ourselves as humans in relation to other animals. This may say much about some people's need to dominate animals as well as other people's desire to care for animals. Whatever it is, I am not sure that, as a culture, we have the necessary resources to talk well about this phenomenon. Our inability to even spot our own inconsistencies is glaring. Many of us decry striking an elephant with an ankus, yet we ignore the process that made it possible to chew, swallow, and digest cows, pigs, and chickens. Surely, in terms of violence, nothing is more brutalizing than the systematic power structures that enable us to process, package, and sell cheap flesh. We are, it seems, a very confused society when it comes to animals, and that often plays out in terms of how we views zoos. To quote Hal Herzog, "Some we love, some we hate, and some we eat."[6] To this I would add, "and some we care for in zoos."

To be sure, zoos evoke all kinds of emotions. The reactions that zoos elicit from people are as varied as the animals within them. They attract animal rights protestors as well as university professors attempting to learn more about who we are in light of what zoos represent. Zoos can inspire people to become conscious of their complicity in the destruction of natural habitats, yet they can also inspire people to see animals as nothing more than exotic entertainment—a mere commodity to be visually consumed. Much of this comes in response to what people find at zoos. Often, zoos have habitats that are too small, or habitats that have been designed with the viewer in mind rather than the one being viewed. Animals may be traded at whim from one zoo to the next to fit whatever niche is demanded. While some animals live longer lives in zoos, others who will never thrive in such environments live shorter lives. There are also quality of life concerns. Most animals in zoos are better fed than animals in the wild, but at what cost?[7] At the risk of sounding anthropomorphic (and what other language can

6. This is the title of Herzog's highly insightful 2010 book.

7. "Better fed" may be a problematic way of putting it. Many zoos feed their animals so "well" that, like many North American humans, they're obese. Dieticians and nutritionists are beginning to play an important role in zoos to make sure the animals are as healthy as possible.

I possibly use?), some of the animals in zoos are miserable, just as some of the animals in the wild are miserable. Of course, and conversely, some of the animals in zoos are happy, just as (I imagine) some animals in the wild are happy. I find myself, therefore, as an animal advocate, trying to locate resources from those who are proponents *and* opponents of zoos in an attempt to find a realistic solution that takes into consideration the vast complexity behind the problem of vanishing and captive species. We have to ask ourselves basic questions about not only why animals are in captivity, but how our understanding of animals has led to their captivity (necessary or otherwise) and how their placement in zoos continues to shape our perspective on them. It is by no means clear that the average zoo visitor walks away thinking that zoo animals are ambassadors of a species in need of saving, though they could think such thoughts. It is incumbent upon zoos to take the necessary steps, to support their claims of education and conservation, as, I fear, zoos may be one of our last remaining gateways to the wild. In some cases, zoos are the only remaining places where some animals can even exist at all.[8]

Of course, much of our experience at a zoo happens before we even arrive. We have certain expectations and make certain presumptions about what we think we are going to discover prior to our discovery. At the same time, many people often come away with a whole host of learning experiences they didn't imagine possible. One of the most rewarding zoo experiences I ever had was when I took my parents to the North Carolina Zoo in Asheboro, North Carolina. Part of the reason my mother never visited the zoo, despite her working in Asheboro for seven years, was her assumptions about the living conditions of their captive animals. She considered it tragic that gorillas and Artic foxes were living in Asheboro. I told her that most curators, keepers, and zoo directors would certainly agree that Asheboro is not the ideal home for any animal who is not indigenous to the Piedmont area of North Carolina. Nevertheless, I suggested that she may want to try to understand how some of these animals arrived there in the first place. I explained that there was certainly no lack of inadequacy at any given zoo but that what contemporary zoos are trying to do, at least as part of their mission, is to spread the important news of wildlife conservation. In some cases, what folks are doing in various zoological parks includes a concerted

8. From Partula snails to Micronesian Kingfishers, there are more than thirty species of animals that exist only in zoos. Due to the diligence of conservationists and their breeding and release programs, some of these animals are actually making a comeback in wildlife parks.

effort to keep certain species from going extinct. Reluctantly, my parents conceded and finally visited their first zoo. For them, the experience was an eye-opener. The majority of the animals they encountered they had never even heard of—much less ever imagined seeing. Given the North Carolina Zoo's emphasis on education, they also learned about the varying degrees of concern for each animal (from "Least Concern" to "Near Extinction"), how the expansion of humans throughout the world has led to the premature extinction of countless species, and, more importantly, what we can do in order to save those animals and habitats that remain. Such a learning experience is not easily replicated in a classroom or on a television commercial. There's something about seeing an animal up close that can inspire the sort of passion to save that animal that otherwise may not be present. I can write article after article about the plight of bongos, for instance, but many people will remain indifferent—or at least not care enough to actually do anything for them. However, bring those same people behind the scenes, allow them to feed a few bongos, and suddenly they may have just fallen in love with an individual animal that, only moments before, they didn't even know existed.

I certainly do not mean to provide a sentimentalized account of our personal experience in an effort to justify the existence of zoos. I am well aware that other folks visit zoos and see nothing but misery. I tell this story for one simple reason: to demonstrate that one can go from visiting a zoo to acting to save endangered and threatened species. In my mother's case, that meant becoming a supporter of the World Wildlife Fund. I can attest to the fact that her sudden concern for animal conservation was directly due to her visit to the zoo. That visit even led both my parents to reimagine their thoughts on the good of creation, its precarious state, and the absolute gift that is creation. Though, as pious souls, they've heard a lifetime of sermons on the good of creation, it was that particular visit that revealed to them a world far larger and more diverse than they previously imagined. They came away asking questions about what we can do to save animals that, only one day earlier, they had no idea even existed. If nothing else, and tabling all of the controversial aspects that constitute a zoo, I cannot help considering their attitude *following* their visit to the zoo to be a good thing.

As I just stated, I am not suggesting that a few feel-good experiences warrant and justify the ongoing captivity of animals. Obviously, zoos do not always have such an effect on people. I am more than aware of this reality. While serving as a Keeper's Aide in the Virginia Zoo, I probably heard everything a person can possibly hear about zoos from visitors. Every time I met someone while wearing my zoo uniform or told someone that I was doing research on zoos, I was quickly told, unsolicited no less, why that person either loved or hated zoos. It was shocking how few people ever understood that their complaints about zoos were nothing new to me. Most of the complaints I heard were complaints that many who work in zoos also make. Speaking for myself, as a person who has been privy to the inner workings of a number of zoos, I have seen the good, the bad, and the really good and bad. I am often horribly conflicted as to my own thoughts on zoos. I find myself playing both sides of the game. When I am around zoo advocates, I am constantly stating what's wrong with zoos. When I am around zoo opponents, I am constantly stating what's right with zoos. It is easy to be conflicted in relation to zoos when you know more about them than what you can find on YouTube.

Like many other people, I love and loathe zoos. I lament that they need to exist, but I am often grateful that they do exist. I am more excited, however, about what they can *become*. Their potential to become places of genuine refuge for the world's dying inhabitants is immense, as is their potential to become the kinds of biological parks that increase our knowledge and awareness of how we, as humans, are one of the greatest enemies of the planet. While Sweeney is correct to emphasize the individual nature of a visit to the zoo, I think that zoos also have the potential to provide a communal experience. It is a communal experience that goes beyond what we experience with other humans. While it is true that sporting events bond us to cities and universities, zoos have the potential to bond us to the entire animal kingdom. While it is certainly the case that zoos have often represented a mastery over nature, a reflection of our ability to control and practice ownership of it, it is not necessary that they continue to function in such a manner. They can grow into something much more. They have the potential to put us in our place in terms of who we think we are in light of the rest of creation. We should, and must, demand that zoos begin to concern themselves with what they say about us just as much as what they say about their inhabitants.

A Conversation with Greg Bockheim on the Place of Zoos

Zoos teach us a false sense of our place in the natural order. The means of confinement mark a difference between humans and animals. They are there at our pleasure, to be used for our purposes. Morality and perhaps our very survival require that we learn to live as one species among many rather than as one species over many. To do this, we must forget what we learn at zoos.

—DALE JAMIESON, *MORALITY'S PROGRESS*

For the latter part of this chapter, I have included an interview with Greg Bockheim, executive director of the Virginia Zoo in Norfolk, Virginia. I have known Greg for several years and he has been a credible and accessible resource. More importantly, however, his zoo career spans the globe and includes working with animals ranging from cobras to elephants. He has worked in zoos in Australia, Great Britain, and the United States. He has also done much in the way of field research, which included the study of gorillas at the Durrell Wildlife Conservation Trust in Great Britain. For these reasons, I thought it important to allow a person who has dedicated much of his life to zoos to speak for zoos. This way, you can read his responses to my questions and think about how those responses either do or do not do justice to the place of zoos in our society.

TRIPP: What would you say is the chief role or purpose of a zoological garden?

GREG: I would say it's to give people an opportunity to marvel at the spectacular—the spectacular nature of other living animals. In a zoo, visitors are able to take that in through all of their senses: sight, smell, and in some cases touch. I think that the specific role is to inspire a kind of "wow" about what's around us, specifically about the kind of animals we are normally not going to see or hear.

TRIPP: Many zoologists and conservationists say similar things when they talk about the sciences being driven by a sense of awe. Where do you hope that awe—or as you put it, that moment of wow—takes your visitors? Where do you hope it leads them?

GREG: I hope that it makes the environment, and all the animals that live in it and constitute the environment, important to them—perhaps in a way they didn't originally envision. Our hope is that by being in the presence of the spectacular, it inspires a sense of care for those animals, for all of wildlife, and for the land and water that makes such life possible.

TRIPP: That sounds like a conservation-based strategy similar to that made popular by Steve Irwin. Granted, he certainly had his fair share of critics. Irwin argued that part of his calling, something he often referred to in a religious vein, was to enable people to fall in love with animals in the hope that those same people would want to save those animals and their habitats. He wanted people to see, smell, hear, and, when possible, touch other animals. He thought it would create in them a sense of love toward those animals.

GREG: Sure. It's simply an easier matter to inspire people to become concerned about what they do know as opposed to what they don't know. It's a little more difficult to get people behind saving something of which they have no direct or immediate knowledge. Part of what we can facilitate is providing the kind of knowledge that inspires people to learn more about these species so that they can do something with that knowledge.

TRIPP: I see that plan happening here with bongos. You are doing work with this critically endangered species in order to breed and release them back into what remains of their native habitat, correct?

GREG: Right. And you're less likely to inspire people to care for bongos if all they see is a commercial, an advertisement in a magazine, or something on a website. But if you can actually see bongos, if you can come into their presence and just be amongst them, then you're far more likely to do something about preserving what is left of their species and their habitat than if you just read an article about them. I doubt that most people who are coming to the zoo are going to spend a whole lot of time reading books on each individual animal or on wildlife conservation or on the loss of habitats that leads some animals to zoos and sanctuaries. There are certainly some who will do those things, and maybe more so after their visit, but many people may not ever think to visit a website for, say, bongos. But they can come here and be wowed by them. That, in and of itself, is part of our purpose. We want to help facilitate the kind of experience that leaves a person awestruck. We think that can produce the kind of mentality that desires to protect and care for the various species that we are currently losing at a rapid and unprecedented rate.

TRIPP: Part of what you are saying, if I am hearing you correctly, is that if you can inspire people to marvel at the animals that populate the zoo the hope is that those same people will become very conscious of how human activity has often been disastrous for these same animals throughout the world.

GREG: That's certainly part of the hope.

TRIPP: I am not sure that many zoo critics are aware of this particular hope, and that unawareness is certainly understandable. Zoos have had, to put it lightly, a rather turbulent history. The state of zoos, however, in just the past few decades, has really improved in terms of issues related to animal welfare, enrichment, natural habitats, emphasis on education and wildlife conservation, as well as breeding and release programs. Thinking about the progression of zoos, what particular areas do you see that must change or improve in order for zoos to be what they need to be for those inside and outside of them?

GREG: I think zoos have to get the word out about who we are, what our mission is, what we stand for, as well as the art and the science of the zoo business, especially in terms of how we manage animal populations and gene pools. The big obstacle is how do you get that message out there? How do we present that message so that people will understand it or will even listen to it? Some critics think we're just out here trading animals because they think it's just financially viable or we don't like the animals. We move animals around in order to preserve and protect that gene pool so that the odds of keeping these animals alive, of keeping certain species from going extinct, are increased. We do a lot of work with other zoos, and we're doing all of this work in the field as well. I think the big challenge, among others, is how we educate the public in terms of why what we do is important and why they should care.

TRIPP: I imagine that's difficult, as the average zoo visitor is probably not coming here because they are intrigued by the biological politics of bongo gene pools.

GREG: Exactly. Most folks are not here to see or learn about those aspects of what we do. And the same thing goes for some of our critics, who are also not interested in learning about those aspects of our purpose.

TRIPP: I recently met with the Education Specialist at The Lemur Center at Duke in order to talk about these kinds of issues. The Lemur Center houses certain species of lemurs that are not found anywhere else except in Madagascar. Talk about dealing with small gene pools. Suddenly, you realize the importance, especially in light of the next thirty to fifty years, of these conversations.

GREG: Yes. It's a serious problem for a large number of species. To be honest, it's not looking very good for a lot of animals—hence the absolute importance of education.

TRIPP: In terms of education, one of the criticisms often leveled at zoos is that they pay lip service to being places of education while remaining, primarily, places focused on entertainment. Certainly the two need not be mutually exclusive. I have no idea why something that can be entertaining, fun, and interesting cannot also be educative. Yet, critics continually point out that, despite the efforts of zoos to educate the public, the majority of people who visit zoos come away, perhaps on a subconscious level, more with the impression that these animals are imprisoned in order to be entertainment for us. That is, these animals are a spectacle that one can enjoy while having a soft drink and some popcorn as opposed to developing concerns about biodiversity and habitat conservation. How do you respond to those kinds of criticisms?

GREG: First of all, while our animals are managed, they are, of course, inside of some kind of barrier. Many animals in the wild, those that we deem to be safe from humans, are safe precisely because they are inside some kind of barrier. Look at the agricultural circle around the mountain ranges of Africa. Those gorillas[9] cannot come out of there anymore; there are human barriers there. Those areas are protected and supported through funding to preserve the land so the animals will be safe. I really think populations that are outside the knowledge of humans and human-constructed barriers are not safe. Even, for example, our own crab and oyster populations here in southeast Virginia. Would we fish them out if there were no rules, if they weren't managed? We probably would and then we'd move on to the next thing and start consuming it. There have to be places owned by conservation groups that purchase land in the wild or help the governments of those countries protect land where it's some of the last habitats for those animals or animals in captivity. Those barriers make the animals a bit more safe, even in terms of those gene pools, and then we have to do the best we can to protect this land because it's not looking like the world is suddenly going to turn around and take care of itself. I don't envision that people, in mass numbers, are going to suddenly take care of the wilderness or habitats around them—at least not in any way that we can be hopeful about all the disappearing species making a recovery. Some of the animals we have here in the zoo are a reminder of what we have had in the past, in some of these disappearing habitats, and perhaps some of them will be able to make a return—assuming we find ways to save habitats. This, of course, means that those habitats will have to be tightly managed. But translating that message to zoo visitors is difficult unless they are paying careful

9. The mountain gorillas of central Africa, the two remaining populations of which are confined to national parks in Uganda, Rwanda, and the Democratic Republic of Congo.

attention to your signs, your graphics, the keepers giving tours, the train conductor driving through the zoo, and so on. The knowledge is there, but it requires that a visitor be open and curious about that knowledge. There is some responsibility on the visitor to want this knowledge; we are not going to force it on her. The zoo is what I often refer to as soft recreation. It is an entertainment experience where we are there to offer people a moment to relax and enjoy themselves as opposed to being a place that takes a hard line and forces the kind of experience on visitors that they may not welcome, or may even dissuade them from returning. Now, in that regard, we do offer educational programs, programs I deliver, programs that the curators and keepers deliver, and I think all of those can convey a message, but they are really only a small snippet or a sound bite of the larger picture. You hope you can get that one sound bite across, so that visitors do learn and take it in, and this encourages them to care about the animals and their disappearing habitat.

TRIPP: That zoos function as a place of leisure seems to be part of their appeal. I'm interested in how zoos have functioned, historically, in cities. They offer this interesting sort of green space. Granted, it's a green space filled with elephants, rhinos, sloths, and tamarins, but it's the kind of space where zoos have discovered that you can't just beat people over the head with this sort of knowledge and hope that they will come back for more.

GREG: I think you're right. This is a green space. I think if you're just looking at a typical zoo visit, part of the reason people visit is to find a bit of an escape. It is entertainment, but we place a very strong emphasis on education, and we think the experience itself can be educational. To answer critics about what people really take from here: I don't know how many people are going to come in here and suddenly desire to become a wildlife conservationist or a biologist. That certainly does happen. We have folks who work here, as well as in the field, because they were influenced to care about such things due to their growing up around a zoo. But while that is great if we can inspire that, I don't know that the primary goal of any zoo is to necessarily create future biologists. We should certainly be in the business of creating within people a strong concern and care for other animals and the environment, but I don't know how far that goes or exactly what that will always look like.

TRIPP: I want to go back a second to what you were talking about in reference to gorillas having these barriers and how the barriers protect them. I often think about how the barriers here between zoo visitors and the animals are really symbolic of what's taking place all over the world. It seems that the barriers, even those in a zoological park, are as much about protecting the animals from humans as they are about protecting humans from the animals.

GREG: I think in some sense that's correct. I have this great picture of [zoologist and author] Dian Fossey, and they're chasing the gorillas back into the mountains. Yet, I can't help thinking, "Oh no . . . this is how it is now. There's not enough room." They have to chase the gorillas back into the hills in order to protect them from humans. I feel great sorrow for those particular gorillas, because they don't have any idea of what's happening. Most of the animals you have in zoos are born in zoos. They're familiar with the barriers, the keepers, and the diets. Due to the training and the enrichment, those animals are going to be calmer and relaxed in their environment. But take a situation like the one I mentioned with Fossey: these gorillas are walking right into danger and they don't even know it. They're sitting ducks. At least most of the animals in captivity were born in captivity. Many of them only know their particular routine, which greatly reduces the level of stress for those animals.

TRIPP: In terms of stress, you often hear about how stressful life is for animals in captivity. Certainly there are numerous species that do not thrive in captivity, as you find very classic stereotypical behavior in some animals such as elephants as well as collapsed dorsal fins of captive orcas. Yet, levels of stress in captivity and the wild are not always so easy to determine. There are a lot of variables at work. Was the animal born in captivity? Did the animal originate in a different environment? How does one determine the stress level of wild animals compared to captive animals? My wife's graduate thesis dealt with testing stress levels in feral horses, and stallions really have it rough in the wild. It's no picnic for them. Indeed, a lot of species, especially social animals, maintain high stress levels in the wild. I'm certainly not making an argument for captivity over life in the wild, or that we cage animals because we are concerned about their stress levels. I'm only noting that with some captive-bred animals, the stress level may be lower than in those in the wild. This certainly does not justify breeding animals in captivity or keeping in captivity animals who exhibit clear signs of stress due to their captivity, only that some of our assumptions about stress may not be as scientific as we imagine.

GREG: When I was recently in Africa we were watching these gazelle graze and every few seconds their heads would pop up looking for lions or any other kind of danger. They were constantly on the watch. "What's coming at me? Who is stalking me?" They would then take a few seconds to eat and go back on the search for predators. It was never-ending. The constant fear of being killed was never-ending. I was thinking to myself, "Nobody is filled with glee out here." They're just on guard for fear of being eaten by any number of animals. And I'm out there at night and I see sixteen elephants pass by on the savannah and in the distance I see the lights of the city. Here we are, in this giant country, but, in actuality, you're on a postage stamp in this giant country, where these animals are "allowed" to live. That's not a good feeling, because you can see it all coming to an end. This is all going to be over someday.

TRIPP: Do you think that there is any hope left for the wild, at least in terms of natural habitats unharmed by humans?

GREG: No. Not much.

TRIPP: Because many groups, such as Born Free, stress that our focus should be on protecting animals in their natural environment rather than showcasing them in captivity. How do you address their emphasis on governments placing funds more in the hands of wildlife conservation rather than on the maintenance of state-funded zoological parks?

GREG: I would absolutely agree that if there are small populations of animals in small remaining habitats that most of the support or funding for the conservation of saving that species or habitat should go to the country of origin or to that particular location. For example, the Guam Kingfisher and those populations are being decimated due to the introduction of the brown snake. We should put the majority of our resources into establishing reproduction centers there where we can build captive environments, as that is what it's going to take to protect the birds from the snakes. In the meantime, we also focus on rebuilding their populations while reintroducing them into their own land. This is an ideal move because the birds do not need to be transported out of the country. I would like to think there would be enough people who would be proud enough of the animals within their own land to want to participate in just such a task. The problem is, there are so many places in the world where there is not enough funding or training, whether it's in nutrition or animal husbandry, for this to always work. Speaking pragmatically, there are just so many limiting factors. So, part of what we want to be about is to be a place where we can take care of animals, help rebuild their population and, if possible, release them back into their native environment. If those kinds of things can happen, then I think there is reason for hope. Of course, for that to work, it will require a concentrated effort from many different groups.

TRIPP: On that note, speak about how people who attend zoological parks—or, specifically, the Virginia Zoo—are directly contributing to conservation.

GREG: The best way I've found to raise conservation dollars that we can then spend supporting great programs for animals in the field, or the scientists studying them, is by adding a fee to our membership prices. Four dollars of each membership here goes toward conservation. If we have twelve thousand members, well, you can do the math. We're raising close to $50,000 to contribute to the field. For me, that's the easiest no-brainer. I think you're not going to raise nearly as much money if you're just asking for it out on the grounds. We also have an "add a dollar to conservation" project at our concession sites, [and] there's our gift shop, as well as the money in the behind-the-scenes tours that goes toward conservation. It also goes into our continuing education fund. A percentage of the latter fund goes toward keeper research and conferences, where the information they learn goes directly into the ongoing care of the animals. Hopefully, in turn, that education makes its way to the visitors. All of this helps out with the bigger picture of wildlife conservation. I think zoos play a vital role, among many roles, for contributing to the big picture, and we do this well when we do what we can in conjunction with other groups and organizations.

TRIPP: We have numerous animal advocacy groups, various animal rights organizations, zoos, aquariums, and sanctuaries, all staffed by people who are, for the most part, genuinely concerned about individual animals and entire species of animals. I have colleagues working with PETA, as well as with smaller various animal rights organizations, and what I have often tried to do is bridge the gap between those groups and those who work in zoos and conservation centers. Unfortunately, we often fall into that trap of thinking that our way is the only way. Part of what I want to do is forge alliances between various animal organizations. Such an alliance could simply revolve around care and concern for animals. How do you envision bridging those gaps and even trying to work with other organizations concerned about animals that may be philosophically hostile to zoos?

GREG: Part of it is very simple: We need to listen to each other. Like you said, there are so many people on all sides that just don't know what the other is about, either because we haven't listened or we haven't communicated those things well. We are just a few miles away from the headquarters of PETA and I've recently learned a lot about their mission. I don't think they're an organization that would be against us. I think they're against bad zoos and the poor care of animals. That's something we can agree on. I think it would take the leaders of the organization talking and coming together to formulate a shared mission that helps animals and helps wildlife. I think it is that leadership coming together to discuss and put into action some sort of mission because, look, life's too short. The planet's already so messy, and it is only in working together that we're going to have a significant impact. We all need to collaborate on creating a vision that we can all work toward together.

TRIPP: Have you done anything specifically in hopes of making that a reality? Have you connected with PETA?

GREG: I have given the Director of Animals in Entertainment, as well as their legal department, a number of tours. Since then, one of their people has left in order to work with the Humane Society of the United States and she has set me up with their Virginia Coordinator. They were here for our hospital groundbreaking. I'm fully willing to somehow work together. It's doable.

TRIPP: What occurred on those tours?

GREG: Dennis [Lead Keeper] brought them through the elephant barn in order to see the elephants as well as what we do with them. That was the first tour we gave them. And you know, we were like, "Are we ready for this? Because here comes PETA!" [Laughs] So, that was kind of cool. We actually spent more time talking about what it means to have a pet than anything else. What was so great about that tour is that I really didn't know PETA well at all. I just didn't know anything about them. At the same time, they didn't know much about what we're doing, and so it was a mutually beneficial conversation where we both came out of it understanding so much more about the other. I think that's why we've had a pretty solid relationship with them. I think we really could work with them once we get to know one another and what it is we all stand for. Perhaps we could come up with a common goal. I think it would be an amazing thing. Let's stop fighting one another, wasting all of that energy, and pull our focus toward helping one another. It could be incredible. Of course, there are extremes within both organizations that could be an obstacle, but it doesn't have to be that way.

TRIPP: One final question: What do you think zoos say about humans? What does a zoological park say about those who create them and visit them?

GREG: I think zoos say that we are very curious, especially about that which fills our senses. We're curious about that which exhibits living behaviors, and part of that may be that we are curious about ourselves. This may explain the overall fascination with other primates, though I think we are, overall, a curious species and zoos reflect this curiosity. We are interested and invested in living, breathing creatures. So, for both good and bad, I think zoos reflect this curiosity. What we have to ask ourselves is this: Where will our curiosity lead us and will it serve the needs of the planet?

INTERLUDE: The Gospel of Dudley

I n Yann Martel's novel *Life of Pi*, the protagonist, Pi Patel, explains how
he views the sloth as one of God's witnesses:

> A number of my fellow religious-studies students—muddled
> agnostics who didn't know which way was up, who were in the
> thrall of reason, that fool's gold for the bright—reminded me of
> the three-toed sloth; and the three-toed sloth, such a beautiful
> example of the miracle of life, reminded me of God.[1]

Pi is often critical of agnosticism. He imagines that lifelong agnosticism
represents a decision never made. He likens it to a sort of paralysis. As
a believer, he finds more in common with atheism than agnosticism. The
atheist, Pi thinks, has at least rendered his best bet and is living his life
based on that decision. Yet, despite Pi's derision of "muddled agnostics," he
likens his on-the-fence colleagues to an animal that reminds him of God.

Perhaps, for the agnostic, that's a compliment.

Pi discusses what he considers to be the holiness of a sloth and how
such holiness comes from being in the world differently from others. In
this sense, Martel's character understands the very basic meaning of the
term *holy*. In Hebrew, the word *holy* refers to being set apart. Pi views the
sloth as an animal that is set apart from other animals based on one key
practice: her inactivity. Pi describes the sloth as an animal that, even at its
most active (sundown), would hardly be considered a go-getter. If threatened, the sloth is barely able to cover twelve to fifteen feet in a minute. With
such movement comes a great expenditure of energy. The sloth, therefore,
has adopted a different approach to the world, and it may very well be her
greatest trait: the ability to go unnoticed.

1. Martel, *Life of Pi*, 5.

36

If only those of us in the family *Hominidae* would take note.

You would think that in a world of dangerously fast predators, the sloth would be easy pickings. Yet, the sloth can survive even in hostile surroundings, partly because of her aforementioned ability to go unnoticed. She blends into her environment. However, this is not what makes the sloth such an intriguing animal to Pi. After all, countless animals survive by being able to blend into their environment. It's basically a staple in the animal kingdom. Stick out and you're not going to last very long. Rather, what interests Pi is what he understands to be the manner in which the sloth is at peace with her environment. This slow, sleepy folivore, who always seems to have a smile on her face, provides Pi with the sense of being in the presence of a meditative yogi akin to "hermits deep in prayer, wise beings whose intense imaginative lives were beyond the reach of my scientific probing."[2]

Having had the good fortune of spending a significant amount of time with the Virginia Zoo's thirty-three-year-old two-toed sloth, Dudley, I have to admit there is something both mystical and monastic about sloths. Their ability to appear almost unconcerned, unfazed by their surroundings, strikes me as the kind of attitude that numerous saints in a variety of religious traditions have often nurtured. Given that their concern is often otherworldly, many ascetics adopt a rather detached approach to the world. They see a different kind of world and attempt to enact it. Sloths, like many of these saints, also tend to see everything differently. By "differently" I mean that sloths see everything upside down. Therefore, they do most everything upside down. They fight, have sex, eat, and give birth all while in an upside-down position. The only time they do see the world right side up is when they come down from their tree, approximately once a week, in order to defecate. Though we're not entirely sure why sloths risk predation by descending from their homes for this particular task, one prominent theory has it that they do so in order to help nourish the trees that shelter, feed, and basically make life possible for them.

I feel there is a lesson to be learned in there somewhere.

Perhaps what is most intriguing about sloths is their amazingly small ecological footprint. Maybe it has something to do with their seeming otherworldliness or their apparent lack of concern with getting things done, but they leave a small footprint. They also play host to many other forms

2. Ibid.

of life. Moths, beetles, fungi, and algae all take up residence on—often—a single sloth. The inverted fur of a sloth is an ecosystem in and of itself.

Now that's an environmentally friendly animal.

As far as the sloth being analogous to a monk or a yogi, that may or may not be a stretch. The sloth's connection to lifelong agnosticism is not entirely clear to me either—especially given how Pi immediately suggests these creatures are a "beautiful example of the miracle of life."[3] Regardless, it seems not a half-bad idea to imbibe the virtuous lessons taught by the sloth. The sloth desires to go unnoticed, to avoid conflict, not to draw attention to itself. Sloths have the incredible ability to nourish their own local environment and to not take more than what is necessary. This enables them to sustain their own lives and the lives of those around them. They also provide a home for a host of other species. The sloth is an animal whose very body nurtures the lives of others. All of these attributes strike me as a gospel in and of itself. The sloth is most certainly good news for creation.

You may just wish to avoid hanging out at the bottom of their tree.

3. Ibid.

3

Freedom's Just Another Word For . . .

I know zoos are no longer in people's good graces. Religion faces the same problem. Certain illusions about freedom plague them both.

—YANN MARTEL, *LIFE OF PI*

As I write this chapter, the Smithsonian National Zoological Park is coming under harsh criticism for a number of issues. News outlets and animal activists are faulting them for poor animal care, criticizing them for insufficient space in various habitats, discussing injuries keepers have received from animals, pointing out animal escapees, as well as questioning how it is possible that a Przewalski's horse, a member of a critically endangered species, broke her neck. CBS ran a brief snippet asking, "Are there animal care problems at the National Zoo?"[1] The obvious and quick answer is, *of course* there are animal care problems at the National Zoo. There are going to be animal care problems at any organiza-

---

1. See Atkisson, "Are There Animal Care Problems at National Zoo?"; Bekoff, "Endangered Przewalski's Horse Breaks Neck"; and Lawrence, "Report Shows Animal Care 'Severely Lacking.'" While people were quick to criticize the National Zoo for "allowing" a Przewalski's horse to die, few people pointed out that the zoo is directly (and almost solely) responsible for saving the Przewalski's horse from extinction. It is one of the few agencies in the world doing anything for this endangered species.

tion whose mission includes the care of animals. The problem with the way CBS and many other critics are stating their criticism is that they could say the same thing about any wildlife center, conservation center, or sanctuary. The problems will differ only in degree based upon the resources and intent of each place that houses animals. For instance, in terms of injuries, you're going to find them anywhere animals are kept. That's unavoidable. I've met caregivers at sanctuaries who were permanently maimed in their work with rescued animals. A caregiver was even killed several years ago at the famed Elephant Sanctuary in Hohenwald, Tennessee. As is obvious, animals rarely discriminate between their various forms of captivity. It doesn't seem to matter to many animals whether you are keeping them for entertainment purposes or have rescued them from a facility that keeps them for entertainment purposes. Whenever you work with or care for animals, regardless of the context, injuries are practically inevitable.

In terms of issues regarding space and habitat, sanctuaries vary as much as zoos. While, for instance, the Elephant Sanctuary in Hohenwald provides far more space for their elephants than any North American zoo, I've visited sanctuaries that make some zoos look like the plains of the Serengeti. Indeed, compared to the North Carolina Zoo's twenty-two-hundred-acre park (with more than five-hundred-acres providing living space for the animals), some sanctuaries look like prisons. Some sanctuaries I've visited could fit, along with all of their animals, in the space that the North Carolina Zoo offers to just their giraffes. Recently, a caregiver at a large cat sanctuary said to me, "Tripp, I wish we had heated rocks for our lions and pools for our tigers." This person was referring to what the Virginia Zoo provides for their large cats. While this sanctuary could only offer "cat" houses inside small enclosures surrounded by metal chain-link fencing, the cats at the Virginia Zoo have spacious lots, large heated rocks, pools, and the ability to move between indoor and outdoor habitats. If you were to compare the habitats at many zoos with, for example, the space provided by some sanctuaries, most anyone, including the people working at those sanctuaries, would choose, for their animals, the space offered by even some of the smallest accredited zoos. This is neither to defend zoos nor to denigrate sanctuaries. I only point this out because every facility with captive animals must be held responsible for its treatment and care of those animals. One cannot assume that a sanctuary provides better care, a higher level of comfort, and more space than a zoo simply because it is called a sanctuary and not a zoo. I have generally discovered that those facilities with the most resources are the ones providing the most adequate space and care for their animals. This is certainly not to knock those people doing everything they can to provide for their animals on a limited budget or to suggest that they love or care less about their animals. I am only noting that many animals benefit when the institutions responsible for their care have greater financial resources.

Even the finest of science-based facilities that focus primarily on conservation still have animal care issues. For instance, Duke University, host to the Jane Goodall Institute Research Center, runs a wonderful facility called the Duke Lemur Center. Just like any other facility that houses animals, they, too, have problems. While they have habitats and enclosures that, in some cases, are much better than some zoos (including an incredible outdoor facility), they also have habitats and enclosures that are not as spacious and as enriching as some zoos. They, like the National Zoo, even face issues with animal escapees. On my tour of the Lemur Center, we discussed a recent escape made by two male lemurs. Upon recovery, those particular lemurs were no longer allowed to roam the electrified-fenced grounds offered to the other lemurs. Their particular confinement is, now, strictly indoors.[2]

Does this make the Lemur Center a bad place? Of course not. The work they are doing for the survival of lemurs is more substantive than any other facility outside of Madagascar.[3] I'm only pointing out that there are animal care problems anywhere there happen to be animals. This is not to suggest that zoo critics are wrong for pointing out the faults of zoos. Such criticism, if constructive, is what makes an institution better. We owe it to all animal care facilities to remain vigilant and critical of them with the hope that such vigilance produces better conditions for the captive animals. I'm only suggesting that you could, and should, ask the same questions of any place that cares for animals. Sanctuaries and science-based wildlife centers, therefore, should not be excluded from criticism, nor should zoos be viewed as the only facilities that house animals. Sanctuaries, wildlife centers, circuses, biomedical research facilities, pet stores, breeders, and pet

2. About two months after my visit, a solitary red-ruffed lemur escaped and was captured in a person's garage. My guess is that he is probably not roaming the grounds anymore.

3. The Lemur Center is the only university-based facility in the world that studies prosimian primates. They host the largest colony of endangered species of lemurs (the majority of which were born on site) found anywhere in the world. Their work for lemurs is unrivaled.

owners all keep animals captive. They do so for many different reasons, but the animals remain, nevertheless, captive. Of course, not all forms of captivity are equal. Given that so many animals live in captivity, it's important that we ask certain questions about the potential good of captivity juxtaposed with the assumed good of freedom. That is, can captivity ever be good in light of the cost of freedom that the captive must pay?

The Pride of Baghdad

However paradoxical it may sound, the truth is actually this: the free animal does not live in freedom; neither in space nor as regards its behavior towards other animals.

—HEINI HEDIGER, *WILD ANIMALS IN CAPTIVITY*

During the 2003 invasion of Iraq, U.S. soldiers stumbled upon something for which they were wholly unprepared: a liberated zoo. Perhaps the word *liberated* is not quite accurate. Under government orders, the Baghdad Zoo had been abandoned by its caretakers and was in total chaos. The captive animals found themselves caught in the midst of a human war and were paying a heavy price for being in the wrong place at the wrong time. Thieves had looted the zoo (with a bear exacting some vengeance on three of the looters), while some people, perhaps thinking they would give the animals a fighting chance, freed many of the animals. However, the majority of the zoo population died of starvation and dehydration. Of the approximate seven hundred animals that were in the zoo, only around three dozen were still alive by the time U.S. forces infiltrated it. Seeing the helplessness of the remaining animals, the soldiers became temporary zookeepers. They found ways of transporting large amounts of water to the remaining animals and made difficult choices about how to keep the large carnivores alive (often by sacrificing smaller animals close to death). The involvement of the soldiers was, of course, only temporary. Their role as zookeepers had an expiration date. Someone else had to step in for the sake of the remaining animals.

Working around an endless amount of bureaucratic red tape, the South African conservationist Lawrence Anthony, popularly known as "the Elephant Whisperer," began the process of rebuilding the zoo. The work was difficult and fraught with all kinds of issues a zoo in his homeland would not have to address. Though many of the Iraqis attached to the zoo were grateful to the U.S. for using their own resources to rebuild the zoo, there remain all sorts of political issues that accompany a situation in which an international team offers aid. The zoo belongs to the Iraqis, not to Anthony or the U.S., and Anthony was very sensitive to this reality. Anthony was there to help the Iraqis rebuild their zoo. He wanted to make sure that the remaining animals had an adequate home.

Due to concerns for animal welfare, an important question was raised: Which remaining animals, if any, should be released into a private reserve and which should remain in Iraq? In particular, there were some intriguing international concerns, stemming from conservation organizations in South Africa, over the fate of Uday Hussein's six lions (three adults and their three cubs). Since those particular lions did not, technically, belong to the zoo, Barbara Maas of Care for the Wild International argued that the lions should be placed in a sanctuary.[4] With the aid of SanWild Wildlife Sanctuary, they would eventually be released into a protected reserve where they could live as lions should live: free and unencumbered by the trappings of their artificially constructed environment.

On paper, it sounded like a really good idea. Who wouldn't prefer the lions roaming and napping in their home environment? Convinced of the eventual relocation, Maas boarded a plane to Baghdad in order to oversee the transfer of the lions. The possible relocation became something of an international sensation. Newspapers in various countries were jumping on the story, running headlines such as "Free at Last" and "Return to the Wild."[5] Again, on paper, it looked like a no-brainer.

There were, however, multiple problems. First, there was the unavoidable stench of Western imperialism. The possible removal of Baghdad's lions by Westerners was not well received. The lions had become a source of pride (forgive the pun) for the Iraqis, and even the hint of their being sold or given to non-Iraqis led to death threats against those working in the zoo. Many Iraqis felt that the zoo officials, their fellow Iraqis, were selling out to the West. The political complexity of such a move was simply underestimated by the good people wanting a better life for the lions.

Though Anthony agreed that several of the zoo's remaining lions needed to be released into a more suitable environment, he was worried about the safety of those who would permit the release to happen. He feared that, ultimately, the entire rebuilding project would come to a halt over this one issue. If so, it would result in the numerous remaining animals being

4. For the full story, see Anthony and Spence, *Babylon's Ark*.
5. Ibid., 205.

euthanized. Everything changed, however, when a second major problem with the potential release of the lions came to light: the adults had been declawed.

In order to avoid being scratched, Uday had had the adults declawed. Anthony and Maas were initially unaware of their declawing. Anthony was almost relieved because he knew there was no way they could be released. It is not that he didn't want them to have better lives; he was just concerned about the possible repercussions of the lions being forcibly removed. In truth, Anthony wanted them to be relocated. He simply felt that their relocation could only happen with the full consent of the Iraqi zoo officials. Without their consent, the results could be disastrous. It was a risky situation for everyone involved—human and nonhuman.

Maas, however, was undeterred. According to Anthony, she remained adamantly in favor of the relocation of the lions. Despite the fact that the three adults had been declawed, she argued they still needed to be moved. When confronted by the reality that the lions would not be able to hunt for themselves, when told that the lions would starve in the wild, she posited a different scenario: the cubs, she argued, would hunt for their parents.[6] As you can well imagine, her comment was met with complete incredulity.

Anyone who knows anything about animals in the wild, or even in a wildlife preserve, understands that the slightest disadvantage is, more often than not, an immediate death sentence. To be sure, this was no slight disadvantage. The cats did not have claws. Given that there are no free lunches in the wild, these lions, if not first killed by other lions, would slowly starve to death. The notion that the cubs would be able to successfully hunt for their parents is baffling. Yet, this is what happens when the best of intentions, coupled with a romanticizing of abstract conceptions of freedom and nature, override reality. It would simply be cruel to place lions that lack claws, not to mention any experience in the wild, in such a situation. The move may make zoo opponents feel better about themselves, but the price of freedom for these lions would most certainly be a cruel death.

The lions were not the only animals Maas wanted to relocate. There was a brown bear named Saedia whom she wanted to send to a sanctuary in Greece. In the sanctuary, Saedia would live out her remaining days free from human contact. As with the lions, the plan sounded great on paper. How could anyone not want a better life for the bear? They were even going to remove Saedia's cataracts so that her sight would be restored (a luxury

6. Ibid., 211.

animals in the wild rarely receive). One of the vets, however, thought it was a bad idea to relocate Saedia. Despite the fact that this veterinarian was very critical of zoos—to the point, it seems, of finding little warrant in their existence—he claimed it would be cruel to relocate Saedia into the wild. She was thirty years old and had spent almost her entire life in captivity. Given that the average life span of a brown bear in the wild is twenty-five years, Saedia was geriatric and would desperately struggle if suddenly cut off from human contact. Anthony reflects on this situation:

> Those with little knowledge of the natural world think of a bear retiring as a human would: in well-deserved comfort after a life-time of toil. In reality, Saedia was so old and so traumatized from the war she probably wouldn't survive the sedation or journey. She also would possibly be frightened out of her wits if she was set free at her advanced age. Her security blanket, heartbreaking as it was to admit, was the zoo and the handlers. Freedom was just a word.[7]

For Anthony, the word *freedom* had become meaningless. In light of the stark reality facing the declawed lions and the bear, the word would be used to make a number of humans feel better about themselves, but it would most certainly spell a long, suffering death for the animals.

We have made a fetish of the word *freedom*. We attach unrealistic at-tributes to what freedom is, what it represents, what it can and cannot do, and then force this word on all other animals. It is precisely for this reason that, contrary to Anthony, I contend that freedom is not just a word. Free-dom is a mythos. It is a story. It is a highly contentious word we force on others, including ourselves, even when it is clear that we are not even sure what it is we are saying when we say it.

It is for this reason that I find Anthony's conundrum with the lions so intriguing. The situation easily lends itself to the exploration of our ide-alized conceptions of freedom and liberation. This is not to suggest that spaces for exotic animals free from human intervention are not ideal, only that our reasons for thinking such spaces are ideal may suffer from a rather misguided understanding of life in the wild. After all, very few of us live in anything that remotely approximates that which we demand for other animals. I'm thinking there is a good reason why, despite our borderline idolizing of freedom, very few of us actually have any idea, or want to have any idea, of what it would be like to live in the kind of freedom we so readily prize for other animals.

7. Ibid., 212.

The Pride of Baghdad Part II

The order you enjoyed may have come at a price … but I'm sure you remember the cost of chaos.

—BRIAN K. VAUGHAN, *PRIDE OF BAGHDAD*

In his graphic novel *Pride of Baghdad*, Brian K. Vaughan explores various ideas related to freedom and captivity. Based on the true story of what occurred at the Baghdad Zoo, Vaughan attempts to think through what it may have meant for the animals to suddenly be liberated. He wants to know if the price for such freedom is a price most animals, including us, would be willing to pay. Set in the war-torn city of Baghdad, *Pride of Baghdad* follows the lives of four lions, inadvertently liberated from the zoo by the war, who are attempting to unlearn captivity.[8] Amidst the chaos of bombs dropping all around them, they experience something they have never experienced before: hunger, thirst, chaos, and fear. These four lions are now experiencing that which non-captive animals have always experienced, and they are torn on how to think about it. Vaughan focuses on the inner turmoil faced by these animals as he attempts to depict what it means to have to find food, water, and shelter every single day, all while attempting to avoid the many animals, including humans, out to kill you.

Vaughan's fictionalized account of the liberation of the Baghdad Zoo reminds us that animals in zoos, unlike those in the wild, have no fear of predators. They have no concern as to where they will sleep or what they will eat. Their every need is addressed by highly skilled people who have been trained to meet those needs. This is not something Vaughan romanticizes; rather, it's just a basic reality of life in captivity. For Vaughan, the questions that come up in light of the four lions' newfound freedom include the following: Which life is better? Which life is more secure? Which life is psychologically more satisfying? More importantly, what sort of resources do we employ to answer those difficult questions for other animals? Vaughan utilizes the four lions to serve as various voices making divergent arguments about what constitutes a good life in light of our conceptions of freedom and confinement. In the process, he muddies what we once thought were clear waters when we speak about freedom, especially when speaking about freedom for other beings that do not share our language and concepts.

8. Vaughan, *Pride of Baghdad*.

To be sure, Vaughan is by no means making an argument for the supe-riority of animal captivity. If anything, Vaughan seems to find the presence of zoos highly problematic. After all, these lions would not even be in this situation if they had never been brought to Baghdad. Vaughan, however, thinks our conceptions of freedom are too simplistic. It's easy to romanti-cize freedom when you don't have to kill for your food or worry that the basic elements of nature might kill you. It's a sham to wax poetic and nos-talgic about freedom as we swipe our debit cards to pay for food, clothing, and shelter. It seems that the people who most want animals to roam freely in the world, as if the world in all her nature and splendor is some sort of benevolent entity just waiting with open arms to care for her long lost chil-dren, are those people who have never experienced the terror and anxiety involved in having to constantly battle hunger, fatigue, and other animals just to survive from one day to the next. There's a very specific reason why so many species, if not the majority of them, have to birth such huge num-bers of progeny: most of them are not going to survive. It's an achievement for most animals to even make it to the point where they can reproduce. Anything after that is just sheer dumb luck coinciding with the fit surviving longer than the unfit.

This is not to suggest that, as an act of charity, we round up the world's animals and put them on display. That would be grossly missing the point. If I am reading Vaughan correctly, he merely asks us to reflect on what kind of preconceived notions we entertain about a word as loaded as *free-dom*. By discussing the potential harm and freedom that stems from a life lived in captivity, Vaughan is obviously drawing analogies to our use of *freedom* as understood under a liberal political regime as juxtaposed to the governing body in Iraq. He wants us to ask what it means to live a life that is constrained and confined, but free of the stress of having to obtain the basic necessities of life. Is there a sense of security that accompanies a more controlled environment? For example, in the U.S. we persistently fight and argue over anything we deem constrictive of our freedom. Should we be free to carry guns wherever we want? Should airport security be free to strip-search us? Should the government be able to monitor our every phone call and e-mail? What are the potential trade-offs of living in a more policed world versus a less policed world? Is the kind of security gained by a more restrictive environment worth the dangers of a less restrictive envi-ronment? How would we possibly know given that none of us approximate anything that looks like a life of freedom (if by freedom we are referring to the kind of freedom we think other animals should enjoy)? Everything about our human world is controlled. What we refer to as civilization is rigidly constructed, managed, and continually maintained for fear that true freedom might actually break out. Everything is as strictly managed and tightly controlled in our world as it is in zoos. Perhaps that's why so many of us don't like zoos. Unlike our world, zoos do not hide the management. Indeed, they pride themselves on it. We, however, seem to enjoy the illusion that our world is less managed than theirs, so we demand that other animals live in a completely non-controlled environment. I'm not saying that's hypocrisy, I'm just noting that what we often demand for other animals is something few of us would ever entertain for ourselves. We ask that other animals live the kind of lives that would terrify us. We mask this reality by referring to it as natural "for them."

Does any of this mean that I think lions should be taken out of their natural habitats and placed on display for the amusement of affluent humans? Absolutely not. I do not think that Anthony and Vaughan are opposed to living lives outside of walls, cages, and locked doors. I think if I share anything in common with Anthony and Vaughan it's that we simply demand more clarification of what it is we are talking about when we talk about freedom. This is especially important when it comes to other animals that do not share our language and forms of life. For it is their well-being, not ours, that should serve as the locus of any conversation about why we house animals.

The Conservators Center: The Pride of North Carolina

If a lion could speak, we could not understand him.

—LUDWIG WITTGENSTEIN, *PHILOSOPHICAL INVESTIGATIONS*

To gain more clarity about what it means for animals to be free, I postponed my search in philosophy and literature in order to discuss these questions with various people who operate sanctuaries and conservation centers. I wanted to talk about freedom with those people who keep animals captive for the sake of those animals. One particular place that captured my attention was the Conservators Center located in Burlington, North Carolina.[9] Cofounded by Executive Director Mindy Stinner and CEO Douglas Evans,

9. For more information, see their website: http://www.conservatorscenter.org/.

the Conservators Center specializes in providing permanent homes for large cats. Though they have become a forever home to other species as well (including binturong, lemurs, and wolves), the Conservators Center focuses on providing shelter for tigers, lions, servals, and other exotic cats who were previously in inappropriate or, in some cases, appalling situations. What is even more interesting, I discovered, is that the Conservators Center collaborated with the U.S. government to provide a home for two of their tigers at the Baghdad Zoo. For these reasons, I asked Mindy if she would allow me to interview her for this book. Mindy happily obliged. Unfortunately, I have had to reduce our numerous conversations, face-to-face chats, and e-mail correspondence to just a few pages' worth of material. One thing I was sure not to leave out, however, was Mindy's comments on how we should think about the good of freedom as juxtaposed with an animal's confinement. Her account is quite provocative.

TRIPP: Why did you create the Conservators Center? What do you see as its purpose?

MINDY: In the early 1990s I was working for a nearby facility that bred rare carnivores and occasionally rescued animals. Of course, at the time, I was very young, outspoken, and opinionated, and I questioned many of their practices and habits. This eventually led to my dismissal, which was a severe blow to me. I decided that if I loved these animals, these species, so much, I should do something about it. I couldn't bear the thought of working for someone else who might tell me I had to leave, or that one of the animals I cared about most was being sent away to a place I might think was not up to par. I decided instead to work with friends who had also parted with my previous employer (a sanctuary for large carnivores) to found a new organization with a three-part mission: education, conservation, and rescue. Our early days were filled with decisions about location, species focus, whether we would ever open to the public, and how in the world we would pay for all this. As the plan evolved, my partner, Douglas Evans, and I were fortunate to be able to move to our current location, generously donated by his mother. We determined that at our outset we would plan to take small animals off-site for educational programs, would assist with some rescue work in our region, and would develop a network of facilities to help establish a breeding program for some of the smaller animals.

Rescue and placement work are very important. A responsible owner looking for a new home for his animal needs resources. A family zoo closing after fifty years needs a home for the animals that have been in their care, especially those with no resale value because of their age or condition. Government agencies need support to allow successful confiscations of animals kept in substandard conditions, and we choose to support the confiscation actions because poorly kept animals at any facility make our entire industry look less professional.

As we researched existing breeding programs for the species we felt qualified to manage, we discovered that a great many species are not managed by the largest zoos. A coordinated breeding effort is a major undertaking and involves a lot of habitat in zoos and other facilities. Most zoos must keep a varied collection to attract and appease visitors. Privately funded facilities have the option to specialize in select types of species and manage them in larger quantity. For example, a zoo might have room designated for two to four wild cat species, usually kept as pairs or singles, and at least one of which tends to be a charismatic big cat like a tiger. A facility like ours can house many more of the same species and can streamline daily husbandry specifically for their needs. On a relatively smaller budget than most state-funded zoos, we house more than thirty big cats and twenty-seven small cats.

We have chosen to focus our breeding program on smaller species that are underrepresented or absent from large zoo collections and are not in other coordinated breeding programs. Smaller animals are less expensive to house properly and to feed than their larger counterparts. We have been selective about who we have chosen to coordinate with for breeding programs, since it is important to be able to trust the people we work with. We are also not interested in creating surplus animals that end up as someone else's rescue. Our policy is to put animals on breeding or educational program loans instead of selling them to help ensure they are always in excellent homes being managed as they should be.

As the Conservators Center has evolved, it's become clear to us that education is the most important aspect of our work. It is a wonderful thing to rescue an individual animal. I have been forever changed by knowing each and every one of the amazing animals we have here. Everyone feels good about a rescue or placement who comes here and thrives. But in the end, saving an individual does not save a species.

These animals do, however, serve as ambassadors for their wild cousins. Meeting them and learning about them helps our visitors understand the importance of preserving these species where we can in the wild, and of maintaining a healthy population in qualified facilities to serve as future outreach animals.

When we can help visitors make a connection with an individual animal in a way that really moves them, we know it will encourage a change in that person's behavior in a way that can benefit the species in the wild. When Thomas Lion stands before a person and meets his eyes, then starts vocalizing his air-vibrating "OOF!" that person feels that connection. He becomes an instant lion advocate. Our tour guides are well trained and are required to work with our animals in order to be able to answer all kinds of questions about them, but the animals speak best for themselves.

TRIPP: Many animal advocates often argue for the role of sanctuaries over zoos. I often find such a sentiment naïve; you know as well as I do that there are great zoos and bad sanctuaries, and bad zoos and great sanctuaries. Do you see the role of sanctuaries as something that can go hand-in-hand with the place of zoos? Do you envision your facility more as a sanctuary or something altogether different? That is, as a conservatory, how does it differ from a zoo or sanctuary?

MINDY: We call ourselves an educational wildlife park and have worked hard to avoid the label of zoo or sanctuary, since neither is an accurate description of what we do. I think of us as being more like a museum learning experience combined with zoo animals, each of whom has his or her own story.

Zoos have traditionally helped each other with surplus animal placements, breeding needed animals for sale, and absorbing animals from closing facilities. Due to the rise of sanctuaries with a big cat focus in recent years, there has been a lot of information disseminated that is sometimes not completely accurate. Some sanctuaries rescue animals at their own expense from truly bad conditions, often at the request of government officials. This is an important role that many zoos have historically played now being largely absorbed by the newer sanctuary industry.

Zoos are not always nonprofit, and most need the animals they house to be self-supporting through admissions pricing. Big and flashy variety helps guarantee a well-run zoo the ability to pay the bills. They have issues with paying for too many of the same species on exhibit, and older or ill animals are generally housed off exhibit (if not humanely euthanized), costing money while bringing in no profit.

If a sanctuary is willing to take them in and cover all their expenses, any business-minded zoo owner would be delighted. No one enjoys euthanizing an animal who may have many years left just because they do not have the appearance or behaviors that make them ideal for exhibit. Zoos in most other countries euthanize surplus animals, even if they are perfect young specimens. That is not considered as acceptable in the U.S., in part because available space in a qualified sanctuary is one appropriate option as a home.

Exotic pets needing placement in new homes do not create enough volume to support a sanctuary for, say, just big cats (I'm not qualified to address sanctuary needs for other species). Some sanctuaries assist with confiscated animals that had been illegally owned or improperly cared for. Most sanctuaries fill up from other businesses including zoos and circuses closing, downsizing or placing out surplus animals, and retiring older animals or animals that have physical or emotional issues that don't make them ideal for public display. Some even take in animals retired from research labs or from other sanctuaries that have failed to stay financially stable. As long as these other businesses exist, there will be an excellent use for sanctuaries.

Sanctuaries that take animals from certain situations—retiring photo booth animals, for example—are actually supporting the industry they rail against. Some places breed what they can afford to house or have another great home for, and use the funds raised from photo experiences with the public to help support those animals. A few places overbreed to have enough young animals to fill their needs without much consideration for where the animals will end up living.

While it is unpleasant to think of tiger cubs in overcrowded conditions at the place that used thém to raise funds, a federal inspector who learns of those conditions will cite the owner until the situation is corrected. Visitors who see animals kept in conditions they do not approve of will not continue to patronize that business. Between citations or even fines and lost business, eventually owners will have a financial reason to change their behavior.

Here in the U.S., zoos and sanctuaries have created a sort of symbiotic relationship backstage, while in public each looks down at the other a little for having different priorities. A zoo may have a more beautiful exhibit, and a sanctuary may be able to house a larger volume of animals less expensively. Honestly, each should support the other in that each does best what the other cannot.

The perception of a sanctuary as a place where throwaway animals come to live in desperation while the managers beg for money in commercials featuring Sarah McLachlan music is part of why we have not defined ourselves as a sanctuary. We do help with rescue work and critical placement requests wherever we can. If we choose to take an animal on, I am betting that the public will support our decision by backing it with their wallets.

The public expectation of a zoo as a park where some animals happen to live is not what we are about, either. I admire a lovely zoo but believe that the educational aspect of what we do is critical to help make change, and not all lovely zoos provide effective educational experiences.

We have made some financial sacrifices to ensure every experience here happens with a tour guide or a stationed docent, and that is simply part of our philosophy. In reality I think we encompass some of the better qualities of both a zoo and a sanctuary, though we will likely never have multimillion-dollar exhibits and will always be limited in what we can commit to rescue ourselves. I am willing to give up the extreme end of the spectrum of success measurement for each in order to fill our own somewhat unique niche.

TRIPP: What do you see as one of the biggest obstacles to the ongoing preservation of big cats? What can we do to avoid their possible extinction?

MINDY: People are overtaking the earth, using up its resources and covering the surface with our homes, businesses, resource harvesting, and garbage. Until we have controlled the explosive growth of the human population, or we have committed to managing our resources more sustainably, we will continue to drive other species into extinction in the wild. Eventually all of the "wild" will be some form of managed park.

Hopefully, these parks will protect at least sizable and sustainable chunks of ecosystems that can function with the level of management we have the science to provide. However, any contained space will have issues sustaining certain animal populations, such as top predators. They typically need a lot of room to roam and hunt without damaging their ecosystems, and they are not great about acknowledging man-made boundaries like the edges of parks. Isolated areas mean limited and isolated populations of big predators. In order for such an area to be sustained long term, new genetic material must occasionally be introduced.

Park managers can arrange the exchange of animals to help facilitate longevity, and even the possible use of sperm or embryos stored in cryogenic banks may be useful for maintaining diversity in some species. Ultimately, though, animals maintained out of the wild, in facilities like ours and in zoos, will be what allows these species to be maintained in the remaining semblance of the wild.

This is a regrettably pessimistic view of the course of the future, but I think we have enough science behind us to see it coming, even if we don't have a plan for how to change it yet.

TRIPP: Could you tell me a bit about your cats that went to the Baghdad Zoo? Could you talk a bit about the politics of making that happen?

MINDY: Sending tigers to Baghdad was an exhausting but rewarding experience. We had been hearing rumors that people within the government were seeking tigers to send to Baghdad for a couple of years. At first we ignored the rumors because we didn't feel it was safe enough to send them. Eventually we got a phone call asking if we might have an interest and we began a very long conversation. We wanted to be sure the cats would be as safe as one could reasonably expect, that they would have a steady food supply and good veterinary care. We read up on what we could find about the zoo from before the war, to get an understanding about its stability and how it was enduring under the regime change.

Eventually, I got back in touch with the U.S. Department of State representative in charge of this matter, who put us in touch with veterinarians who had been to the zoo and could give us a frank assessment of the situation. For a variety of reasons including age, condition, and temperament, none of the cats we had were good choices for sending overseas. We launched a search among the private zoo community seeking two unrelated, young, well-socialized tigers not necessary for any established breeding program who could come stay here with us while we started the long, slow process of applying for permits and arranging transport.

We were very fortunate that a woman we had met not long before had acquired a zoo that had a large population of tigers. She had been downsizing her volume of other species but had elected to keep the big cats as her focus. She had also maintained a relationship with the previous owner so she was able to obtain documentation of the origin of each cat, which was required as part of the permitting process. She was willing to donate the tigers to us for the purpose of sending them to the Baghdad Zoo, though she had as many concerns as we had had about the situation they would be entering. Because she had been in business herself for a relatively short time, it was more likely that we would be able to get the permits to export the cats, so it made sense for her to transfer them to us before we started the process of permit applications.

We housed them here, boostered their vaccinations, filled out a mile of paperwork for permitting, coordinated with the transport team, and talked to a lot of people in the military, the State Department, and the Baghdad Zoo. I completed some deceptively simple-looking paperwork for a CITES (Convention on International Trade in Endangered Species) permit, which allows endangered species to leave the U.S. for international travel. Part of the process involved being listed in the Federal Register as seeking this permit, which gave activist groups who disagreed with our decision to send the cats an opportunity to have their say in a public forum.

Many of the critics had no information to go on except the request itself, and I repeatedly answered questions about the conditions at the zoo. It was the first and only time we have sent an animal to a location we had not inspected ourselves first, which was hard for us. But, having seen photos of them since then, I have no regrets. Doug and I accompanied the tigers in cargo as far as Bahrain, where we transferred them to another plane for entry into Baghdad. A high-level officer who was also a veterinarian took over their care for the short remaining flight, and followed up with us afterwards to let us know how their adjustment was progressing. He has since visited us here, as have many soldiers who saw the cats at the Baghdad Zoo during their time in service.

Tripp: Could you say something about how we often read our own preconceptions about the wild onto the wild? Do you find that most people who visit your facility harbor rather romanticized notions of the wild?

Mindy: I find that often people who have grown up in cities and towns have no concept of what living in the countryside is like, what the predator and prey balance is like in the world around us, or even where their food comes from. Urban gardening projects have helped start to make people more aware of the reality behind some of these issues, but such programs have obvious limitations.

When students arrive at our Center to see the animals, we get a lot of questions about whether we feed them live prey, why we don't house them all together, and why we don't just let them all go. These are all excellent inquiries for starting the discussion we humans need to have, especially with our children, who will inherit the earth in whatever condition we choose to leave it to them.

We are overpopulating the earth. We are using a large amount of natural resources, and often this has unintended or unexpected effects on the world around us. We use fuels and create energy for our consumption in ways that are affecting our entire climate. We clear-cut forests and then the wind carries away our remaining soil. We drink water from wells and irrigate our crops, which we now see contributing to the formation of sink-holes. We change our environment by clearing, leveling, planting crops, removing minerals, and an endless list of other behaviors, each of which has an impact. It adds up.

Everyone who loves animals wants to see them thriving in the wild. Humankind has largely taken that option away from animals in large areas of the world. What we take, we rarely return, and when we do, it is often in such sorry shape that it will be useless for generations of wildlife. When a child asks me why we don't just let our tigers go, I ask them how they would feel waiting at the school bus stop knowing that a dozen tigers roamed free nearby. So why not send them back to India? We pull up a map of the population of India, which pretty much answers the question itself. The few remaining wild places are supporting what they can already, and dumping in new predators to fight over limited food, [who will] try to leave by walking out through populated areas or get poached, will not help the situation.

We also talk about the skills the animals born in human care have developed. I ask the child what would happen if I dropped him off in the countryside, alone. How would he eat? Where would be sleep? How would he find other people? How many of our native plants can you identify as edible? What if you only had a knife—could you kill an animal to eat it? Could you catch something in the first place? Even if you have a fishing pole, you have to find a pond, be skilled enough to bait your hook and catch a fish, and then prepare it so you don't get sick. Would you sleep outside, unprotected from biting bugs or cold weather? Or would you risk trying to burrow into a hole under a tree root ball that maybe already has a resident creature living there? Both children and adults often answer that they would walk until they found a road with people and cars, or a farm with food to eat. Then I say, that is exactly what a tiger who grew up near people would also do.

People who love the idea of nature but have not spent much time in it tend to see it in one of two ways. Either everything gets along in a perfect balance of predator and prey in a pristine human-free environment, where even our young children can romp and play safely (thanks to a great many children's cartoons and movies), or everything is constantly trying to kill everything else, and only the toughest survive. The truth lies between these absolutes.

Animals who live in the wild die much younger on average than those under human care, be it in a zoo, a pet home, or a managed reserve that looks very wild. Most of the animals born in the wild at some point in their lives have come close to starvation, have had parasites that sap their energy, and have endured a serious injury like a broken limb or porcupine quills in the face. They are indeed free to roam where they will, even if it means getting hit by a car or shot when they predate on livestock. They are free to hunt as their instincts dictate and as likely a parent taught them, as long as they can find enough food to eat, are skilled enough to catch it, and something bigger or stronger does not come along and run them off. The toughest and most hardy animals survive, thrive, and multiply. Some of their offspring live long enough to have their own, as well. Most do not. The most adaptable animals are moving into new territory, pushed out by humans into areas they have never had to live in before, often separated from others of their kind by roads and cities they cannot navigate. Truly incredibly adapted animals include those who have found ways to live with people, like raccoons, rats, pigeons, and of course our own pet dogs and cats, who came from wild ancestry. As they are some of the most populous nonhuman mammals on earth, I'd say it has worked out well for them.

TRIPP: While captivity is certainly not ideal for most animals, what do you see as particular advantages to captivity for certain individual animals as opposed to the non-captive animal?

MINDY: No one I know thinks it is a good thing to have a tiger living in a small cage with no connection to the wild world he was meant to live in. So places like ours seek to find the best balance we can provide. From my front window I can see Tonka, an older male tiger, sleeping in the sun on a hammock made of fire hose. There would be no fire hose waiting for him in the jungles of Asia, but he would have a grassy or leafy hummock where he might nap from a good vantage point. Here, he has a hammock instead.

On two sides he has female tigers close to his age living only a few feet away. Neither had an interest in him as a companion, and Tonka has had his share of female companions earlier in his life, so now he seems content to simply know they are nearby. On a third side, about fifteen feet away at the closest point, Tonka has a younger tiger with a giant ego that he can argue with when he feels like it. Both spend time marking their boundaries closest to each other, in spite of the younger male being neutered. With that male tiger lives a female lion who flirts with Tonka on occasion. When she calls out across the acres to all the other lions, often Tonka joins in the calling, as if to make sure he is included.

Our hound dog, Peggy Sue, runs wildly past him several times a day, ears flapping and tongue lolling. Sometimes he ignores her, and other times he pounces in her direction. Tonka's den has two sections and fresh straw as winter bedding. He is never cold during ice or snow, unless he chooses to go play in it, which he sometimes does. Tonka has trees and shrubs around him, providing shade and the smell of fresh greenery from March to November most years. He has a pool he soaks in on hot days—and pees in, sometimes on the same day. He has staff members and volunteers here who have cared for him from the moment he arrived until now, a consistent family of familiar faces who take care of him every day. He moves between sections of his habitat at their request so they can keep his pool clean and his bedding changed. They leave him presents when they visit, including fresh chicken or beef, homegrown peppermint leaves crumbled into a box, a dab of whipped cream, a bit of hay from another tiger's den box.

A year ago Tonka fell seriously ill and was unable to move much or even drink water for several days. Our human community nursed him through it, keeping him hydrated and warm while medications did their job. Today you would never know he had been sick.

Tonka has adoptive human parents who visit him and sometimes bring treats. He knows the sound of their car pulling in from a half mile away. He will sit up, stand up on a high vantage point to look out for them, and begin to pace in anticipation of their visit. They are pretty nuts about him, too.

During events Tonka gets Christmas trees or pumpkins stuffed with meat or wrapped present boxes with whipped cream inside. Sometimes he gets so excited he gets his head stuck in the box while he is licking inside and has to pull it off afterwards. When music plays nearby, he listens, ears always moving, tail sometimes flicking. Tour groups and classrooms of children pass near him regularly, asking questions, laughing, and making the hubbub of people. He watches us all and ponders what he sees. Sometimes he sits up and engages with us. Sometimes napping or splashing water on the tiger next door is more important. It is Tonka's choice.

He will never roam free in Asian jungles or on Siberian plains. He will never be sick or injured and unaided. He will never race after and catch warm, bleeding meat. He will never den up hungry in winter. He will never fight another male tiger over territory or a female, and will not then kill her offspring to bring her back into estrus. He will not die alone and injured, slowly starving and unable to hunt, or by approaching a village of frightened people because they and their livestock represent easy prey for an aging cat. He will not be killed by a poacher for his bones or coat. When Tonka's time comes, he will pass from this life here, in human care, possibly by our hand so that he will not suffer needlessly.

This is Tonka's life with us. Is it better than a life lived free, with all the challenges that entails? Only Tonka can answer that question.

INTERLUDE: The Human Zoo

One of my favorite short stories by H. H. Munro (also known as Saki) is "The Mappined Life." In this story, Munro describes urban life as analogous to a zoo. Often when we hear something referred to as a zoo we are captivated by images of chaos. We tend to think of something that is disorderly or out of control. Zoos, for the most part, are the exact opposite of chaos. Everything in a zoo is tightly managed. Diets, enrichment, exercise, veterinary care, training, and space for animals are all specifically designed, heavily scrutinized, and tirelessly controlled. It is exactly on this latter point that Munro likens urban life to that of zoos—and none too favorably.

The story begins with Mrs. Gurtleberry suggesting that the "Mappin terraces" at zoos are a great improvement on the cages once found in zoos. She claims that the improved artificial habitats provide the visitor with the illusion that they are seeing the animals in their natural environment. This leads her to question if the illusion is passed on to the animals. Her niece astutely replies that it would greatly depend upon the animal in question:

> [A] jungle fowl, for instance, would no doubt think its lawful jungle surroundings were faithfully reproduced if you gave it a sufficiency of wives, a goodly variety of seed food and ants' eggs, a commodious bank of loose earth to dust itself in, a convenient roosting tree, and a rival or two to make matters interesting. Of course, there ought to be jungle cats and birds of prey and other agencies of sudden death to add to the illusion of liberty . . .[1]

The unnamed niece suggests that the very thing that maintains the illusion of freedom, the presence of a predator, is the one element missing in a zoo.

1. Saki, *Complete Saki*, 479.

One of the ways a zoo fails to replicate a natural habitat is by not including that which can kill an animal. Being prey is, for most animals, part of the high cost of freedom. Having the good sense to not include predators in their exhibits, zoos purposely limit the freedom of both prey and predators. Without a doubt, zoos intentionally limit the freedom of predators to predate as well as the freedom of prey to perpetually fear being killed.

For the niece, however, her point has little to do with the freedom of predators and prey. She finds that most animals, even if there is no predator, still seem to imagine that predators exist. It's a form of self-policing that, perhaps, many species, most definitely humans, tend to practice. It is on this latter point that we discover that the niece is not so much interested in ideals of how predation does and does not lend itself to understandings of liberty as much as the manner in which humans seem to suffer from the illusion that, unlike animals in confinement, they live lives of freedom.

Undeniably, the niece finds even the most incredible zoo habitats to be poor substitutes for what the animal is likely to deem spacious and natural, but given that humans have confined their own selves to false ideals of liberty, it is no wonder that the best we can offer other animals is a sad replica of the world that produced these animals. The problem, it seems, is in our own ideals of what constitutes liberty that we read back onto other animals.

Mrs. Gurtleberry suggests that her niece's account is depressing. Mrs. Gurtleberry does admit, however, that while the new exhibits do appear to be spacious and natural, she imagines that "a good deal of what seems natural to us would be meaningless to a wild animal."[2]

Her niece responds that it is on this point that "our superior powers of self-deception come in." She claims, "We are able to live our unreal, stupid little lives on our particular Mappin terrace, and persuade ourselves that we really are untrammelled men and women leading a reasonable existence in a reasonable sphere."[3] She continues by explaining that

> we are trammeled by restrictions of income and opportunity, and above all by lack of initiative. To some people a restricted income doesn't matter a bit, in fact it often seems to help as a means for getting a lot of reality out of life; I am sure there are men and women who do their shopping in little back streets of Paris, buying four carrots and a shred of beef for their daily sustenance, who lead a perfectly real and eventful existence. Lack of initiative is the thing

2. Ibid., 480.
3. Ibid.

> that really cripples one, and that is where you and I and Uncle James are so hopelessly shut in. We are just so many animals stuck down on a Mappin terrace, with this difference in our disfavour, that the animals are there to be looked at, while nobody wants to look at us.[4]

I imagine that it is our most fervent desire to be looked at that is, paradoxically, most appalling to so many of us about zoos. In a zoo, animals are on display. Though many of us protest this kind of exhibition, humans are remarkable in proving, time and time again, via social media outlets and other forms of narcissism, that we are the greatest of exhibitionists. The recluse is the deviant of our species. The one screaming and begging that we look at him or her, while strategically placed, confined, and controlled by the Mappin terrace, is the norm. Unlike zoo animals, however, we are our own captors. Knowingly or not, we orchestrate and participate in our own form of captivity. While the heart of Munro's story rests on the assumption that zoos provide a sort of lifelessness for their animals (an assumption that is both true and false), life in the city, or life plugged into the grid, is hardly any different. We are managed, controlled, directed, self-policed, and, just like in a zoo, enriched by the toys we are taught will enrich us. Munro's assumption is that such a life is lifeless. I would wager, however, that most of us, despite what we may say or think, are quite content with our captivity. Perhaps the only difference between a zoo and life on the grid is that we are our own predators. We protest against the confined lives of other animals—often rightly so—but we demand that they live the kind of lives that would have the average person begging for an Orwellian world. We are a comfortable animal, and rarely do we allow for anyone to challenge our comfort—especially when we refer to it as freedom.

4. Ibid.

Mufasa on arrival at the Conservators Center. What cannot be seen in this photo is his overall poor health, which includes bony hips, an emaciated chest, and long-term hip sores. (Photo taken by Kim Barker)

Mufasa after a few months in his new home. He's a healthier and happier boy. (Photo taken by Kim Barker)

Hope and Riley waiting for what will be a long journey to their new home. (Photo taken by Derek Evans)

Hope and Riley settling into their new life in the Baghdad Zoo. (Photo taken by Bob Sindler)

Dudley looking for some treats. I was more than happy to hook him up.
(Photo taken by Tripp York)

Larry, the emerald boa. You do not want this beautiful creature showing you his teeth.
(Photo taken by Tripp York)

A pair of bongos who are a part of the breeding and release program at the Virginia Zoo. (Photo taken by Tripp York)

Cita and Lisa eating a tree. Notice the house in the background. Surreal. (Photo taken by Tripp York)

4

The Ongoing Task of Adam

Animals come when their names are called. Just like human beings.

—LUDWIG WITTGENSTEIN, *CULTURE AND VALUE*

For those people who claim Christianity as the lens by which they narrate the world, conversations around animal captivity—whether animals in zoos, in circuses, or in our homes, or those animals bred and slaughtered for consumption—must begin with an understanding of animals as depicted in Scripture. The point of this chapter is to briefly explore a few areas of the Bible in order to see if we can draw any claims as to the purpose of animals. If it is the case that humans are those animals who name other animals, we need to examine whether or not our naming is theologically appropriate. We have to ask a very straightforward question: Does our naming of other animals bear faithfulness to the claims made by the Christian narrative?

The Politics of Naming as Proclaimed by a Self-Named Animal

Everything's got a name. It's how we make crap belong to us.

—BRIAN K. VAUGHAN, *PRIDE OF BAGHDAD*

In Gen 2:18–20, God parades the animals before Adam and gives him the challenging task of naming each animal. For those who interpret this passage literally, I can only imagine that a scholar no less than Linneaus would be quite impressed. After all, to name every bird of the air and every animal of the field is no small task. Such an undertaking would require countless centuries. Indeed, it has taken countless centuries, and yet we are not done—the naming continues today.

What often goes unnoticed in this passage is how the ancient Hebrews were, implicitly, attempting to make sense of their relationship to other animals and how it differs from relationship to other humans. Here's the text:

> Then the LORD God said, "It is not good that the man should be alone; I will make him a helper as his partner." So out of the ground the LORD God formed every animal of the field and every bird of the air, and brought them to the man to see what he would call them: and whatever the man called every living creature, that was its name. The man gave names to all the cattle, and to the birds of the air, and to every animal of the field; but for the man there was not found a helper as his partner. (Gen 2:18–20)

For those of us familiar with the story, we know that God compensates for Adam's loneliness by creating Eve. Yet, interestingly enough, this is not God's first response. Rather than, initially, creating another human, specifically one with an XX chromosome, God first parades all of the animals in front of Adam in order to see if Adam can find an appropriate helper.

Despite the potentiality, or lack thereof, of interspecies suitability, God seems to realize, only after the fact, that while many of these animals would prove to be of tremendous help to Adam (imagine where we would be without the donkey, horse, and cow), none of these animals were suitable in what appears to be the most significant sense of the term: reproduction. While I can only imagine the horror Adam must have felt when God initially marched the porcupine in front of him (yet one more reason to forego literalism), the great parade seems bent on reducing suitability to potential mating. This does not, however, eliminate the more important aspect of this text, which revolves around Adam's power to dictate purpose through the act of naming.

As an act of power, our naming of animals confers upon them a particular role. Through the act of naming, we determine an animal's purpose in relation to us, as well as the animal's role on the planet. Our naming of them decides *for* them their meaning. As problematic as this sounds, the naming of other species seems inevitable. I am not sure how we can avoid the process of naming. The question, therefore, is not so much *if* we are going to name other animals, but *how* we are going to name other animals. In particular, are we going to name them in such a way that our naming of them is rooted in how we understand the purpose of creation?

Such naming is not always terribly obvious. We name in a variety of ways, and whether or not such naming is good or accurate may depend upon the primary resources we rely on for understanding that which surrounds us. Minimally, it appears, we name other animals in at least four different ways: We give them scientific names, popular names, individual names, and—what I contend is a fourth manner of naming—relational names.

The scientific names are the Latin designations grounded in a subdiscipline of zoology called taxonomy. Taxonomy is the discipline of classification. You'll often find labels depicting these names outside zoo and museum exhibits that explain how the animal, or relic, is classified.

This manner of classification contains at least two parts: the genus and species (rooted in a larger, hierarchal, tree of life)—the idea being that these words should indicate some of the properties of the animal as well as, possibly, where the animal was first located or who did the locating. A great example of how a scientific name is capable of speaking volumes about an animal is the case of the emerald boa. The Latin name of this gem of a snake is *Corallus caninus*. The latter nomenclature says much about their ferocious bite. I have had the opportunity to gaze at the canines of an emerald boa, and their teeth are incredible. This same snake bit a colleague of mine who happens to be a seasoned herpetologist. The bite and blood flow was impressive. There are anticoagulants in the emerald boa's saliva that make it difficult to stop the bleeding. Fortunately, emerald boas are nonvenomous, so there was no real threat beyond the very painful bite. The point is, anytime you find an animal with *caninus* as part of his or her scientific name, you would be wise to approach such an animal with tremendous caution, if at all.

Of course, many of the scientific names are not always quite so inter-esting. My leopard gecko's scientific name is *Eublepharis macularius*, which refers to a gecko that has eyelids and spots. This is a fairly straightforward manner by which we name. Lest, however, you think taxonomy is the driest of all subjects, a camel spider discovered in Inyo County, California, was labeled *Eremobates inyoanus*, while a salamander discovered in the Long-dong River in the province of Sichuan, China, was called the *Batrachuperus longdongensis*. Taxonomists certainly have their moments.[1]

An animal's second name, their popular name, refers to what an ani-mal is often called. These are the names we most often use for animals that are representative of an entire species. *Cow, horse, human,* and *armadillo* are examples of popular names. To stay with the example above, most peo-ple will refer to emerald boas as emerald boas rather than by their scientific name, *Carollus caninus*.

An animal's third name, if they have one, is their individual name. These are the names we give to each individual of a species. They are of-ten our attempts at personalizing an animal. The name of the emerald boa who bit my friend Dennis is Larry. So, it was not just an emerald boa that bit Dennis, it was Larry who bit Dennis. This naming creates a different vantage point for viewing other animals. It provides more of a historical context while also denoting a personality that, while already present in all animals, makes it more viably understood for the human. Another example would be that of the squirrel monkey pictured at the end of this book. His name is Jeeves. Jeeves is the individual name of a squirrel monkey (the popular name) whose scientific name is *Saimiri sciureus*. Let it be clear, however, it was not simply a member of *Saimiri sciureus* who once pooped on me. It was most definitely Jeeves who climbed above me, took careful aim, and defecated on my shoulder. Though he has his own personality and history regardless of whether or not I name him, Jeeves and I now have a different sort of history together. It is one that I can name as personal, and it provides me with a different kind of context for viewing Jeeves that, I believe, can better suit the needs of Jeeves.

What's the point of these names? The practice of naming is inherently an act of power. We are not simply labeling things; we are labeling life. We are the ones who name planets, stars, plants, animals, rivers, trees, and

---

1. Bright's *The Frog with Self-Cleaning Feet* lists a number of scientific names provid-ing evidence that zoologists may be the most comedic of all scientists. I mean that as a compliment, of course.

other humans. Names are descriptors. They create within us, and others, certain expectations. More importantly, naming functions to classify and categorize the known world. Indeed, what is not named is not known. We need to name in order to know. The problem, it seems, comes from why we need to know and what we plan on doing with such knowledge. That is, how does naming something, therein knowing something, place that named entity into our understanding of the world? How does it place that life form under our power?

To complicate matters even more, there is, I believe, a fourth manner of naming. I refer to this manner of naming as relational naming. This practice of naming revolves around purpose and, specifically, human use. That is, how does our naming of animals somehow dictate the particular relationship that those animals have with us? It is in this fourth manner of naming where we find ourselves on very slippery ground as we narrate, for other forms of life, how those animals are going to exist (or not exist) in this world. We determine, for all other animals, how they are going to relate to us. We also often determine how they will live and die. It is in this fourth form of naming that we exercise our greatest power in relation to other living beings. Therefore, we must closely examine how we practice this form of naming if we are to think and live well with other animals. More importantly, we have to ask ourselves what we are saying about other animals, what roles we are determining for them, when we name them relationally. For example, what are we saying about animals when we refer to them using some of the following descriptions?

- medicine
- cosmetics
- entertainment
- pet
- family
- food
- companion
- friend
- research
- accessories

- broodmare
- stud
- livestock
- clothing
- boots
- belts
- ornaments
- trophies
- art
- collection

The list could go on, but I think you get the idea. While it is not necessarily the case that this kind of naming benefits only the one doing the naming, we can certainly see how it is not always clear how such naming benefits the one being named. We must ask, therefore, who benefits from such naming, and why that matters for how we name animals. The problematic nature of such naming, I believe, is that it tempts us to commodify other living beings. We are tempted to name in such a way that we are always the ones who benefit from this naming. This is not to suggest that wearing leather belts—or, I should say, cows—is inherently wrong; it is only to point out that, by refusing to notice the manner in which we name animals, we self-servingly relegate the rest of the animal kingdom to our own ends. Such naming strikes me, to say the very least, as theologically suspect. In this fourth and, I believe, most powerful act of naming, we decide for each individual animal his or her function in life. If I see a cow and say, "hamburger," I have decided, for that cow, her only purpose. A hamburger exists for no other reason than to be food. Therefore, the cow has no other reason for existing except to be consumed. The *Bos taurus*, the cow, who likely lacks an individual name, is now called meat, and this means that the cow's only purpose is to serve the needs of the ones who have decided her purpose. Meat has no other purpose than to be food. The animal labeled meat is labeled with no concern for the needs and desires of that particular animal. Her future is written by the ones holding the pen. So goes the way of all meat.

My concern about this fourth form of naming is how naming either does or does not reveal what it is Christians claim to think about creation.

The secular animal-activist can agree that how we label animals is of utmost importance, but she will, perhaps, find different tools for how to think about this fourth form of naming. For those people whose faith originates in the Jewish and Christian narrative, there has to be a more faithful manner of naming animals than the names given above. This is not to say that those names are wrong (more on that in the next chapter), only that for those people who claim a common creator, and refer to the Bible as their ultimate source of authority, they have to, at the very least, adopt a more biblical manner of naming animals.

But What Does the Bible Say?

I said in my heart with regard to human beings that God is testing them to show that they are but animals. For the fate of humans and the fate of animals is the same; as one dies, so dies the other. They all have the same breath, and humans have no advantage over the animals ...

—ECCLESIASTES 3:18–19

When it comes to animals, the Bible often seems to provide a rather mixed message. Sometimes God demands animal sacrifices, and sometimes God doesn't. There are rules on how to kill and how not to kill animals. Peter argues that Christians can eat any kind of animal, because he wasn't worried about purity issues, and Jesus feeds five thousand people with a couple of what must have been really, really big fish. If you take only the quickest perusal of animals in the Bible, there seems to be plenty of evidence that they exist for no other reason than to benefit humans. I would argue that such an interpretation is inaccurate.[2] While there *are* some mixed messages about animals in the Bible, there are certainly a few common elements that enable us to render a basic judgment as to how the biblical writers understood the purpose of animals. Listed below are just a few passages that should provide us with at least a very basic idea of how the Bible understands nonhuman animals:

2. For an account that addresses commonly asked questions about animals, as well as the larger environment, from the perspective of Christian thought and practice, see volumes 2 and 3 of the Peaceable Kingdom Series: York and Baker, *A Faith Embracing All Creatures* (2012) and *A Faith Encompassing All of Creation* (2014).

So God created the great sea monsters and every living creature that moves, of every kind, with which the waters swarm, and every winged bird of every kind. And God saw that it was good. (Gen 1:21)

God said, "See, I have given you every plant yielding seed that is upon the face of all the earth, and every tree with seed in its fruit; you shall have them for food. And to every beast of the earth, and to every bird of the air, and to everything that creeps on the earth, everything that has the breath of life, I have given every green plant for food." (Gen 1:29–30)

Then God said to Noah and to his sons with him, "As for me, I am establishing my covenant with you and your descendants after you, and with every living creature that is with you, the birds, the domestic animals, and every animal of the earth with you, as many as came out of the ark. (Gen 9:8–10)

All animals belong to God. (Ps 24:1)

Your righteousness is like the mighty mountains, your judgments are like the great deep; you save humans and animals alike, O Lord. (Ps 36:6)

All the animals in the forest are Mine and the cattle on thousands of hills. All the wild birds are Mine and all living things in the fields. (Ps 50:10–11)

He gives animals their food and feeds the young ravens when they call. (Ps 147:9)

The righteous know the needs of their animals, but the mercy of the wicked is cruel. (Prov 12:10)

But ask the animals, and they will teach you, or the birds of the air, and they will tell you; or speak to the earth, and it will teach you, or let the fish of the sea inform you. Which of all these does not know that the hand of the Lord has done this? In his hand is the life of every creature and the breath of all humankind. (Job 12:7–10)

And should I not be concerned about Nineveh, that great city, in which there are more than a hundred and twenty thousand persons who do not know their right hand from their left, and also many animals? (Jonah 4:11)

The wolf shall live with the lamb, the leopard shall lie down with the kid, the calf and the lion and the fatling together, and a little child shall lead them. The cow and the bear shall graze, their young shall lie down together; and the lion shall eat straw like the ox. The nursing child shall play over the hole of the asp, and the weaned child shall put its hand on the adder's den. They will not hurt or destroy on all my holy mountain; for the earth will be full of the knowledge of the LORD as the waters cover the sea. (Isa 11:6–9)

Search in the LORD's book of living creatures and read what it says. Not one of these creatures will be missing and not one will be without its mate. The LORD has commanded it to be so; He Himself will bring them together. It is the LORD who will divide the land among them and give each of them a share. They will live in the land age after age, and it will belong to them forever. (Isa 34:16–17)

I will make for you a covenant on that day with the wild animals, the birds of the air, and the creeping things of the ground; and I will abolish the bow, the sword, and war from the land; and I will make you lie down in safety. (Hos 2:18)

Look at the birds flying around . . . your Father in Heaven takes care of them. (Matt 6:26)

Are not five sparrows sold for two pennies? Yet not one of them is forgotten in God's sight. (Luke 12:6)

And then I heard every creature in heaven, on earth, in the world below, and in the sea—all living beings in the universe—and they were singing: "To Him who sits on the throne and to the Lamb, be praise and honor, glory and might, forever and ever." (Rev 5:13)

Based on these few passages alone, four things seem quite clear. First, animals do not belong to us, they belong to God. Second, the ultimate purpose of other animals is to not serve us, but to serve God. Third, God cares for all animals, both humans and nonhumans. Fourth, and finally, these animals, just like us, will forever reside in God's kingdom. If nothing else, these four points must serve as a reminder that whatever purpose animals have it is directed first and foremost toward God and not toward us. That very basic understanding alone should be enough to temper how prideful we can be when we imagine the various roles that animals should serve for us. Like all other animals on this planet, our only purpose, as well as theirs, is to serve the One that gives life. Any other speculation about the purpose of other animals must be carefully weighed and measured against their primary purpose.

Practicing Dominion

It is necessary and urgent that, following the example of the poor man [St. Francis], one decide to abandon inconsiderate forms of domination, capture, and custody with respect to all creatures.

—POPE JOHN PAUL II

To claim that human animals and other animals are alike is not to suggest that there are not significant differences between them. Along with biological differences, there are theological differences as well. The Bible refers to humans as beings created in the image of God who have dominion over other animals. This particular passage, Gen 1:26, is often used, oddly enough, to justify the kind of brutality that humans often exercise over other animals. The passage says, "Then God said, 'Let us make humankind in our image, according to our likeness; and let them have dominion over the fish of the seas, and over the birds of the air, and over the cattle, and over all the wild animals of the earth, and over every creeping thing that creeps upon the earth.'" Why anyone would read this and think such a passage somehow condones brutalizing billions of animals a year is unclear to me. Yet, for some people, that is exactly what dominion entails. Over and over again, the first thing many Christians say when you talk about proper care of and hospitality toward other animals is, "But God gave us dominion over the animals." True, but whatever that may mean, it does not mean that we can simply do whatever we want to them. Dominion does not mean that we are allowed to maim, injure, hurt, bully, torture, and destroy any animal who is in our path. It does not mean we are allowed to abuse other animals or ignore the untold suffering we bring to other animals. Dominion does not mean that everything on this planet is unimportant except us humans. It does not mean that we should plunder the earth's resources for schemes of our own devising. Whatever dominion may mean, and it may mean many things, it must indicate the kind of care and concern God practices in relation to creation.

Because I think our dominion is rooted in God's dominion, I am not interested in attempting to dissociate myself from the concept of dominion. I think we are better off attempting to own it. We just need to understand it in light of how God exercises dominion. That is, if we are created in the image of God, if we are to mirror the character of God, then this means that whatever dominion might look like, it has to reflect the manner in which

God exercises dominion in relation to us. This is why Oxford theologian and animal ethicist Andrew Linzey argues that humans do have a privileged status above that of other animals. Linzey claims that, according to Gen 1:26, humans are the servant species.[3] He suggests that as those who bear the image of God we must treat all of creation as God treats us (or, at least, as we want God to treat us). This, I believe, suggests that we must ask one very simply question: What are the central tenets of the Bible? At the risk of being reductionistic, I think we can safely argue that some of those tenets include hospitality to the stranger, care for the poor and the oppressed, an overarching concern for the least of these, and most certainly, God's constant and immutable grace and mercy extended to all of creation. It is here where Linzey asks Christians to go one step further and imagine the concept of dominion from the specific focal point of Christianity: Jesus. Linzey says, "If it is true that the power of God is most authentically expressed in the form of suffering service then we have to ask ourselves radical questions about how we are to understand our own lordship or dominion over nature in general and animals in particular."[4] This means that if Jesus lowered himself, gave himself for the sake of all creation, and demanded that we serve, that we not lord our power over others, that we die to ourselves—and if Jesus is indeed our paradigm for living—then whatever form dominion takes it must look like the crucified servant. That, I imagine, changes everything.

As the image of God on earth, humans have the privilege and burden of appropriately caring for other animals. I do not pretend to necessarily know what that always looks like, only that the primary question we have to ask ourselves is how our treatment of other animals bears witness to their purpose. It is not a matter of whether or not it is permissible to eat meat, attend a circus, or perform medical research on rhesus monkeys; rather, the question primarily revolves around whether or not any of the abovementioned practices enable such animals to bear witness to their specific purpose. It very well may be the case that such reflections will call into question the above practices. I cannot know that ahead of time. I can only know that if I am going to attempt to think theologically with other animals then I need to do so in light of their purpose. While we practice dominion, while we care for that which God has entrusted to us, we have to ask ourselves questions about the manner in which we name other animals in order to

3. For further explanation on what it means to refer to humans as the servant species, see Linzey, *Animal Theology*, 45–61.

4. Ibid., 54.

make clear whether or not such naming is faithful. In order to do this well, as we will see in chapter 6, we will have to think eschatologically. For now, I hope it is enough to simply state that the natural world, in all of its splendor, violence, decay, and mystery, is a world that groans for completion (Rom 8:22). If this sounds a bit odd to you, then welcome to the strange world of the Bible. It is a world, after all, where donkeys talk (Num 22:28), where livestock are covered in sackcloth and encouraged to fast (Jonah 3:7–8), and where Jesus tells us to preach to the whole of creation (Mark 16:15). It is a world that extends beyond that of the tiny and thus far short-lived world of humanity. In Christian thought, there is God and there is creation. We, like everything else, are a part of creation. The only significant difference is that we have been charged with the task of naming and caring for creation. If we are to do this well, then we need to be able to name well. In order to name well, we need a more sacramental understanding of the world that surrounds us, or what Henry Beston refers to as a more mystical understanding of our world:

> We need another and a wiser and perhaps a more mystical concept of animals. Remote from universal nature, and living by complicated artifice, man in civilization surveys the creature through the glass of his knowledge and sees thereby a feather magnified and the whole image in distortion. We patronize them for their incompleteness, for their tragic fate of having taken a form so far below ourselves. And therein do we err. For the animal shall not be measured by man. In a world older and more complete than ours they move finished and complete, gifted with extensions of the senses we have lost or never attained, living by voices we shall never hear. They are not our brethren, they are not our underlings; they are other nations, caught with ourselves in the net of life and time, fellow prisoners of the splendor and travail of the earth.[5]

One thing is certain: a more mystical concept is sorely needed. The only thing I would nitpick is Beston's notion that these other nations are not our brothers and sisters. Biologically, we are related. It is in such relatedness that we can better develop an understanding that could potentially lead us to treat our kin with a more profound level of respect. That it is not just with other humans or even chimps that we share a family resemblance, but that, biologically speaking, we are of the same material as land mammals, marine mammals, and invertebrates, must somehow find its way back into our

---

5. Beston, *Outermost House*, 24.

collective imagination. Such a notion is not simply a biological concept; it is a theological claim as well. According to the scriptures shared by Muslims, Jews, and Christians, God creates all life from soil. It is not simply evolutionary science that claims that humans share the same material origins as other animals; Genesis plainly makes that claim as well. Genesis 2:19 states that God forms out of the ground every beast of the field and every fowl of the air. That which gives life to humans is that which gives life to all animals. All animals, human and nonhuman, share a common ancestry in the earth (a claim made by science and Genesis) as well as in the one who created the earth. Not only is God the shared creator of all life, but according to Genesis and Hosea, God also creates covenants with every form of life. This includes plants and animals, the human and the nonhuman. Theologically speaking, all animals, from the sponge to the white heron, are our kin. This is biological and this is theological. This is the miracle of creation, and we are charged with not only caring for it but also reveling in it. To do this well, we must learn how to name creation well.

INTERLUDE: The Immaculate Conception of Goofy

When a miracle is said to be beyond the expectation of the one who beholds it, the hope in question is the hope of nature and not of grace.

—THOMAS AQUINAS

L est anyone be confused, when I say Goofy, I am not referring to one of Mickey Mouse's best friends. The Goofy of whom I speak is a day-crested gecko. She has, it seems, inadvertently earned her name. Compared to other geckos, something is slightly different about Goofy. Her movements are rather awkward and her eating habits are slow. Her body is fully intact and her blood work suggests she's fine. She's just a bit, for lack of a better word, *goofy*.

It sounds horrible, I know, but I promise you, it's a term of endearment. Truth be told, I never referred to her as Goofy. It's not that I found the name to be offensive or unkind, I just found it to be terribly unimaginative. Instead, I always referred to her as Theotokos.[1]

More on that in a moment.

Goofy's/Theotokos's so-called goofiness, we think, may have had something to do with her lack of a father. By lack of a father, I'm not referring to the absence of a father in her rearing; rather, I'm referring to the fact that, biologically speaking, she has no father. Goofy is the result of parthenogenesis.

---

1. Theotokos refers to the God-bearer, or the one who gives birth to God. It is often used by the Eastern Orthodox, as well as by Catholics, to refer to Mary the mother of Jesus.

She was born of a virgin.

Parthenogenesis refers to the ability of some animals to reproduce asexually. As surprising as that might sound, male fertilization is not required for these animals to reproduce. Parthenogenesis, at least in some animals, appears to be an adaptation that has developed in those species where males no longer exist (or are not viably present).[2] Asexual reproduction has been confirmed in many different species including sharks, reptiles, birds, crustaceans, and various insects.

Parthenogenesis is, theoretically, not possible in humans. Of course, Christianity depicts Mary, the mother of Jesus, as procreating parthenogetically (via slightly different means than reptiles and sharks). When Christians refer to Jesus as born of a virgin, we can only think of such a conception as miraculous. By miraculous, many people seem to be referring to the suspension of the rules of nature, at least as we currently understand them. This very well may be a misunderstanding of the poetic nature of the miraculous. When St. Augustine first formulated his conception of a miracle, he referred to it as that which exceeds our expectations. He refers to a miracle as that "which is not contrary to nature, but what is contrary to our understanding of nature."[3] A miracle is that which extends beyond the capabilities of the one marveling at it.

In a recent debate, the former archbishop of Canterbury, Rowan Williams, and noted zoologist and atheist Richard Dawkins discussed how divine intervention may or may not work in our understanding of evolution. Dawkins and Williams both agree on the basic tenets of evolution and how problematic it is to suggest that God somehow interrupts that process, as if, in Williams's understanding, God did a poor job in the first place and continually finds the need to correct God's mistakes. Williams then goes on to say a bit more about his understanding of the notion of a miracle, in terms of how we name miracles, and what that means in light of the natural world:

> If you think of miracle as those sets of circumstances in which somehow or another the underlying action of God breaks through,

2. This is not, however, always the case. When an Atlantic blacktip shark died during a routine examination at the Virginia Aquarium, the necropsy revealed a pup in her womb. Shark biologist Robert Heuter argues that the presence of only one shark embryo suggests that the fertilization was not based so much around the lack of a male mate as much as it may have been a type of developmental anomaly with the egg. See Goudarzi, "Shark 'Virgin Birth' Confirmed."

3. Augustine, *City of God*, XXI, 8.

breaks through the surface to create something new, I think that's consistent with an underlying stability of divine action.[4]

Dawkins then becomes a bit more pointed and asks how it is possible for Christianity to reconcile its understanding of the natural world with the idea of the virgin birth. In his attempt to explain how it is the case that Christianity has historically understood the possibility of the virgin birth, Williams responds,

> Here you have a long history of preparation for the coming of God in a new way. Here you have a particular life, that of Mary, opening itself up to the action of God in a certain way and then there is an opening. Something comes through, something fresh happens which is not—if you like—a suspension of the laws of nature but nature itself opening up to its own depths—something coming through.[5]

Williams does not refer to Jesus's birth as a suspension of the laws of nature; rather, he sees it as an instance by which nature opens itself up to its own depths. Dawkins expresses bafflement, saying, "I'm not sure what that means," to which Williams responds, "It's poetic language."

I openly admit that it's not entirely clear to me, either, what Williams is suggesting. Along with Dawkins, I'd like Williams to say more. I simply don't understand his description of "nature opening itself up to its own depths" in such a way that I would necessarily know it when I see it. Perhaps, for Williams, that's the point. Perhaps it requires a different sort of training to see it. Perhaps Williams is simply suggesting that in our desire to understand, know, and, oftentimes, domesticate nature, we forget that we are nature. As the great conservation scientist E. O. Wilson suggests, nature is, by its very nature, miraculous. Wilson states, "No words and no art can capture the full depth and intricacy of the living world. . . . If a miracle is a phenomenon we cannot understand, then all species are something of a miracle."[6] This is not to suggest that the idea of a human reproducing asexually is possible or that it happened with Mary; instead, the idea that I believe both Williams and Wilson are intimating is that over and against the fundamentalism attached to knowing the world only through the lens of scientism, there exists the mystery and wonder attached to the recogni-

---

4. See http://www.dailymotion.com/video/xd6d3l_archbishop-rowan-williams_tech.

5. Ibid.

6. Wilson, *Creation*, 55.

tion that, as a part of nature, we are not, ultimately and finally, knowable. Nature is a miracle. Nature will always exceed our understanding and expectations. Nature is a mystery.

No doubt that Goofy/Theotokos is certainly the product of something miraculous called nature. The question I have is, *why* is it the case that some people see nature as miraculous and others do not? Is it because some of us lack the scientific resources necessary for comprehending the depths of nature? Even when something like the Big Bang theory, or cellular replication, or parthenogenesis is explained to me, I don't find it any less miraculous. Instead, I'm filled with awe and wonder. This, in turn, leads me to question *why* I'm filled with awe and wonder. Ultimately, I'm not sure such a question can be answered via the scientific method. I definitely do not think the answer can be explained through the disciplines of theology and philosophy. I'm quite compelled to admit that, in all of our attempts to provide explanations, theologians and philosophers have continually missed the mark. If, indeed, the question is answerable, perhaps it will come through the paths of art, music, and poetry. Unfortunately, as you can tell, I'm certainly no poet.

But nature is poetic.

And Theotokos is the result of such poetry.

5

Captive Flesh (and Their Lovers)

The question is not, Can they *reason*? Nor, can they *talk*? But can they *suffer*?

—Jeremy Bentham, *An Introduction to the Principles and Morals of Legislation*

The greatness of a nation and its moral progress can be judged by the way its animals are treated.

—Gandhi

I once heard a self-proclaimed elephant advocate proudly reciting the above quote by Gandhi. I found it curious that he was quoting Gandhi, for the reason that this person eats animals. I'm thinking he may have missed Gandhi's point. Nevertheless, he enjoyed parroting the quote anytime he felt obliged to let everyone know he supports better treatment of zoo and circus elephants. I, too, consider myself to be an advocate for elephants, but the cynic in me thinks this particular person found it easy to campaign for elephant welfare because such a stance requires neither sacrifice nor a change in lifestyle. To be honest, I do not know of a single person who is not an advocate for the improved treatment of captive elephants. It's kind of a no-brainer. Who doesn't want a better life for elephants? The uninteresting thing about such a stance is that it doesn't really change your daily activities. It doesn't require much in the way of living any differently. It's a pretty easy cause to support. Complaining online about wanting a better life for elephants, or showing up at your local zoo to let them know how "evil" you think they are, isn't a very interesting form of activism. It serves the protestor more than it serves the animals. It requires so little from the advocate, yet it gives the illusion that the advocate is crusading on behalf of captive animals. Such crusading is little more than a self-serving attempt to avoid the reality of life for the majority of captive animals in the United States. There are, after all, only a few hundred elephants in North American zoos.[1] Such numbers pale in comparison to the more than nine billion animals held captive on factory farms. When I asked this elephant crusader how he could square Gandhi's quote with such statistics, or with the cow he just swallowed, he looked at me dumbfounded, rolled his eyes, and then muttered something about how cows are different from elephants. Yes, indeed, cows are certainly different from elephants. Whether or not they are different in a way that allows them to be systematically tortured, beaten, maimed, executed, and turned into food, however, strikes me as a rather unwarranted kind of difference.

Recently, I brought up this same conversation in a class of undergraduates while we were discussing the role of animals in our culture. One of them, a very conscientious student who, much like the elephant advocate, loved Gandhi's quote, agreed that care for some animals does not necessitate care—or at least the same kind of care—for others.

"Fair enough," I said. "That may be quite sensible on a number of levels. But, if we are sticking with the intention of Gandhi's comment, I don't know, especially as a Hindu, that he would be willing to suggest that the life which animates one animal is any different from that which animates another animal—be it a sponge, a mosquito, or a cow."

"Well," she said, "I guess the main difference, on that point, is that the purpose of the cow is to be consumed by humans."

"Not for Hindus."

"Thank God," she quickly retorted, "I'm not a Hindu."

1. There are roughly six hundred elephants in zoos and circuses in the United States. I am not trying to downplay the serious issues surrounding the proper care of elephants in captivity. The existence of elephants in North American zoos is problematic, yet, as previously noted, extremely convoluted. I will return to this point in the epilogue.

"I hear it's an okay way to see the world, but the point is, what you are really saying is that for a couple hundred million cows a year, while their purpose is to be bred and consumed, their actual purpose is to be held captive in the worst possible conditions imaginable where the only relief they have to look for is being slaughtered. Would you say *that* is their purpose?"

This very bright young lady, a self-professed lover of animals no less, thought for a moment, tapped her pen on her desk, and then confidently said, "Yes."

At least she's honest (though I'm thinking she may have missed Gandhi's point, too).

Unfortunately, I have found this sort of attitude to be typical of many people who claim to love animals. Many of these same people, those I have met in zoos, sanctuaries, pet stores, and adoption drives, consider themselves to be animal advocates, yet I have discovered that many of them are only advocates for their preferred choice of animal. Most often this is a pet or some slightly more random animal they have fallen in love with at a zoo. Many of these same people pay little or no attention to the fact that their diets entail a systematic brutalization of animals unheard of throughout all of human history. It's easy to campaign for the humane treatment of animals in zoos and circuses, as that rarely requires any personal sacrifice or change in lifestyle.[2] Yet, ask these same folks to be consistent in their advocacy for the animals bred for no other reason than to be slaughtered, and their heroic efforts are suddenly trumped by their insatiable desire for flesh. As the conservationist of all conservationists, Jane Goodall, states,

> Thousands of people who say they "love" animals sit down once or twice a day to enjoy the flesh of creatures who have been utterly deprived of everything that could make their lives worth living and who endured the awful suffering and the terror of the abattoirs—and the journey to get there—before finally leaving their miserable world, only too often after a painful death.[3]

Goodall is pointing out the inconsistency of self-proclaimed animal lovers who only love those animals who fulfill their own needs. We fool ourselves, and others, when we claim to be pro-animal despite the fact that our diets

---

2. Of course, there are many people who tirelessly champion the improved treatment of animals in zoos and circuses. The above comment is not meant to ignore their own personal sacrifices. I am sure they may even agree with my assessment.

3. Goodall, "Introduction," in Goodall and Bekoff, *Ten Trusts*, xv.

lead to the pain, suffering, and torture of countless creatures. We are, by and large, not animal lovers; we are merely lovers of certain animals.

It is therefore not clear to me how it is possible to discuss animal captivity well if we do not discuss the mass production and consumption of animals. In the United States, we breed billions upon billions of animals, while maintaining their captivity in some of the most inhumane environments ever devised, for no other reason than to eat them. We kill roughly eight billion chickens a year for food. These birds are reared in some of the most merciless surroundings in the world. How can we think well about animals in captivity—whether in zoos, sanctuaries, circuses, or conservation centers—if we refuse to discuss the fact that the number of animals kept and killed *per day* in U.S. slaughterhouses is greater than the number of animals in all of the world's zoos, sanctuaries, circuses, and conservation centers combined? In fact, the number of chickens we kill *per hour* exceeds the total number of animals in all accredited zoos and aquariums in North America. Why are so many of us eager to discuss the supposed plight of captive animals in zoos while refusing to discuss the captive animals on our plates? Is this nothing more than the worst kind of self-serving hypocrisy, or is it just a lack of awareness in otherwise conscientious people?

My point is that those people who advocate for a better life for captive elephants (or any other species) take the easy and inconsistent road if they fail to make the connection between their diet and the welfare of animals such as pigs, cows, fish, and chicken. If you are concerned about animal welfare, remember that the animals we humans chew, swallow, and defecate are, well, animals. As I mentioned to a number of my students, especially those who claim to be animal advocates, rather than masquerading as an animal advocate, perhaps they should be a little more honest and say that they only advocate for the welfare of certain animals. Such a qualifier enables a person to speak a little more carefully and a little more honestly. This also requires that a person come to terms with *why* they care for some animals and not others. I imagine there are very good, legitimate reasons for why we care for some animals and not others, but we should at least be willing to admit that fact. I worry that we choose to love some animals and not others simply because it behooves us to do so. We love dogs because of how they make us feel, we love cows because of how they taste, and, perhaps, we love elephants because they need us to be their heroes. A potential concern about any and all of our relationships with other animals is that, ultimately, whatever it is we do to or for them, more often than not, revolves around how it serves us as opposed to how it serves them. Whether we eat them, wear them, dissect them, or even attempt to rescue them, the motivating factor is often the same: we do it for ourselves.

I do not intend to sound cynical; I am just noting that even the most altruistic relationships we have with other animals are often self-serving. That's not necessarily a bad thing. We just need to be honest about why it is we do the things we do to or for other animals so that we can understand how and why it is that we have the relationships we have with them. This will tell us more about who it is we think we are in relation to other animals, and why that may or may not matter.

It is for the reasons above that I find conversations about our diets pertinent to any conversation about animal captivity. As already noted, factory farms maintain, literally, billions of animals in captivity. This is well beyond the reach of all of our sanctuaries, zoos, circuses, medical and conservation centers combined. I am curious as to why, as a society, we tend to question some of these latter forms of captivity and not our factory farms. Is it really just because food animals are hidden that, by and large, so many of us just do not care what they have to endure? Is it hypocritical for one who eats factory-farmed animals to protest the conditions endured by zoo and circus animals? More importantly, is there a connection between our shared refusal to question the existence of animal captivity for food and our tolerance for other forms of captivity?

The Reluctant-to-Talk-about-It Vegetarian (Am I the Only One?)

I can't count the times that upon telling someone I am vegetarian, he or she responded by pointing out an inconsistency in my lifestyle or trying to find a flaw in an argument I never made. (I have often felt that my vegetarianism matters more to such people than it does to me.)

—Jonathan Safran Foer, *Eating Animals*

I am not a fan of vegetarianism. By that I mean to say that I am not a fan of talking about something called vegetarianism. I especially lack the desire to talk about vegetarianism in the way that people talk about religion, politics, science, or any other ideology. My take on vegetarianism is similar to my take on almost everything else. If you're a vegetarian, that's great. You don't need to tell me about it. You most certainly do not have to tell me why you're a vegetarian. Hopefully, your manner of life will be all the evidence I need to understand why you made that decision. That, for the most part, is also how I feel about religion and politics. If you're a Christian, good for you. You don't have to tell me. As a matter of fact, if you do have to tell me, then you're probably not much of a Christian. Just *be* a Christian. Let that speak for itself. Likewise, if you're an atheist, please, control yourself—you certainly do not have to tell me you're an atheist, nor do you have to regurgitate the litany of preprogrammed reasons why you're an atheist. Just go live it and stop telling me about it. You simply do not need to inform me of your political affiliations, religious preferences, or dietary choices. Just embody them. If I need to know why you do what you do, I'll ask. Otherwise, feel free to keep it to yourself.

It's for those reasons that I am not interested in discussing vegetarianism, or, specifically, why I am a vegetarian. As many of my friends will tell you, except in the case of onions (I'm convinced they're an invention of Satan), I rarely talk about what I do and do not eat. Part of it is I am just not entirely sure how to discuss vegetarianism without coming off as self-righteous (which is already a difficult temptation for me). Over the last few years, I've just decided not to talk about it unless someone else brings it up. And let me tell you, someone always brings it up. Always.

I guess that could be a good thing. At first I thought that most people inquired about it because they were genuinely curious about the diet in terms of health benefits. It is a very curious thing to hear, time and time again, from people who haven't the slightest idea of what B-12 does for the body inform me that their diets are healthier than mine because I cannot get B-12 (which is not true—I get B-12 in spades). Rarely do people who employ the vitamin argument actually care about vitamins; it is often just something many people say in order to justify their own diets. Certainly there are exceptions to this rule, but I have discovered that the main reason people raise the topic is that, for some reason, they feel compelled to justify their consumption of animals in an effort to show me why I am wrong. Perhaps that, too, is a good thing. I am open to the possibility that I am wrong (if there is a "wrong" or a "right" when it comes to being a vegetarian). If nothing else, such opportunities afford me the space to clarify my own dietary habits. Yet, many of my conversations about vegetarianism, whether they are personal or public, seem to stem from how offended some folks are by the idea that another person does not eat what they eat. It's as if my refusal to eat flesh somehow implicitly condemns their consumption of flesh. As I said, I rarely talk about vegetarianism because I am very reluctant to stand in judgment of what other people eat. I know that irks many of my vegan and vegetarian friends, but I am often more bothered by their sanctimonious condemnation of other people's diets than I am by other people's diets. I just do not find it helpful to be antagonistic toward others' choice of diet, partly because I don't think that is the best way of convincing people to examine what they eat. Typically, doing so precipitates a clash of monologues detailing why one person does or does not eat animals. Such conversations are rarely helpful. Yet here I am feeling compelled to offer some sort of explanation as to why I am a vegetarian and what that has to do with animal captivity. I will do my best to keep this as brief as possible, as I do not want to lose sight of why a conversation about vegetarianism is important to any discussion of the end(s) of animal captivity. To be sure, I believe such conversations are more than peripheral to conversations about animal captivity. Our diets directly impact other animals, other humans, and the larger environment. Our health—our very existence—is intertwined with the health of other animals and the health of the earth. Yet so many of us slavishly adhere to unhealthful diets. C. David Coats notes these connections well, and with no hyperbole, when he asks,

> Isn't man [sic] an amazing animal? He kills wildlife—birds, kangaroos, deer, and all kinds of cats, coyotes, beavers, groundhogs, mice, foxes and dingoes—by the million in order to protect his domestic animals and their feed. Then he kills domestic animals by the billion and eats them. This in turn kills man [sic] by the million, because eating all those animals leads to degenerative—and fatal—health conditions like heart disease, kidney disease, and cancer. So then man [sic] tortures and kills millions more animals to look for cures for these diseases. Elsewhere, millions of other human beings are being killed by hunger and malnutrition because food they could eat is being used to fatten domestic animals. Meanwhile, some people are dying of sad laughter at the absurdity of man [sic], who kills so easily and so violently, and once a year, sends out cards praying for "Peace on Earth."[4]

4. I first discovered this quote in Masson, *Face on Your Plate*, 160. It is widely quoted and originates from Coats, *Old MacDonald's Factory Farm*.

Animal Rights to Animal Rites (It's More than Just Ugly)

All the arguments to prove man's [*sic*] superiority cannot shatter this hard fact: in suffering the animals are our equals.

—PETER SINGER, *ANIMAL LIBERATION*

I became a vegetarian when I was a junior in college. A good friend of mine gave me a copy of Peter Singer's *Animal Liberation* and I read it in one sitting. If the purpose of a good book is to change your life, then Singer's *Animal Liberation* is an extraordinary book. I immediately stopped eating animals. I don't know if it was the philosophical utilitarianism (which I quickly overcame) that swayed me, or the images replete with horror and suffering (which I have yet to overcome), but Singer's book was a game changer. Even though I now disagree with much of what and how Singer argues, I appreciate that his book actually changed my life. That, I contend, is good philosophy. Singer's *Animal Liberation* changed not simply how I ate but how I saw the world. Even though, as I just mentioned, I moved away from that which underwrites how Singer reasons, I have never been unable to "un-see" the world he showed me. It's for that particular reason that I really do understand, especially looking back, why freshly minted vegetarians are often so passionate (to put it charitably) about their diets. It's hard work. When you're raised on a diet of animal flesh, and when you're used to frequenting Biscuitville and Chick-fil-A (the quintessence of fine dining in the South), it is not always easy to give up sausage gravy biscuits and chicken sandwiches covered with delicious pickles. Partly this is due to the fact that many people do not become vegetarians because they hate something called meat; rather, they often become vegetarians in spite of their love for meat. I think, therefore, because it is initially such a sacrifice, many vegetarians are quick to be defensive about their stance against the consumption of flesh. Abstaining from animal flesh can be, at first, challenging. Some vegetarians, in their attempt to convert others, will try to persuade you that it is the easiest thing they've ever done. I don't trust those people. You shouldn't either. It certainly does become easier, and it is amazing how quickly it becomes natural. More importantly, it becomes an actual joy to not eat animals. It is its own reward. Nevertheless, it is safe to say that, for many people, the initial process of giving up meat is disruptive. How could it not be disruptive? You are changing something you do two to four times a day, and some folks do not handle the disruption well. The very fact that there are three times as many ex-vegetarians as there are current vegetarians demonstrates this point.[5]

Perhaps another reason for the initial shift to vegetarianism is that we are not, by nature, vegetarians. Of course, neither are we carnivores. We are omnivores. There's not much we cannot or will not eat. Humans are like many other animals on this planet in that many of us have a love affair with eating various species of animals. It seems the reasons why we do or do not eat certain animals, though not always arbitrary (polar bear livers would be a bad choice for anyone), are, in many cases, simply contingent upon what a culture deems acceptable. What we humans eat varies greatly from culture to culture. Many of us in the United States would never eat a dog or a dolphin, whereas some people in Korea and Japan have no problem dining on, respectively, either animal. Some of us see a frozen octopus in a grocery store and our ick factor kicks in, yet those same people may see pig brains and think, "Delicacy!" Some of us consume chocolate-covered insects, ant-covered salads, squid-inked fettucini, shark fin soup, ikizukuri (a fish that is eaten while still alive), as well as, annually, some twenty billion hot dogs. The fact that anyone would eat a hot dog, knowing what is in a hot dog, is evidence that there is almost no end to what we consider edible. For many of us, it all depends on how and where we were raised, how adventurous we are, and, for two of my friends in particular, how much alcohol they imbibed moments prior to choking down live shrimp.

Yet, again, this reveals to us our radical inconsistencies. What is it about seeing dolphins slaughtered in Japan that angers so many of us, while we ignore the fact that we do the same exact thing to cows, chickens, and pigs? Why is the life of a dolphin so much more morally significant than, say, the life of a flounder? Is it a question of intelligence? Pigs are smarter than cats and dogs, yet we slaughter more than one hundred million of them a year. Or is it rather our romanticizing of some species and not others? Ultimately, who is to say which is worse, and what sort of rationality are they employing to draw such a judgment?

In either case, it seems that the morality/immorality of the act is being determined by individual or cultural preference. This is precisely why philosopher Alasdair MacIntyre critiques modern accounts of ethics (which most certainly includes Peter Singer). MacIntyre argues that modern ethics are grounded in little more than our own personal preferences.[6] He claims

5. Herzog, *Some We Love, Some We Hate*, 200–201.
6. MacIntyre, *After Virtue*, 6–51.

that modernity locates knowledge of good and evil in the individual self, which, inevitably, concedes authority to the will of each individual. To put it plainly, what this means is that the claim that butchering dolphins is more morally suspect than butchering cattle is rooted in little more than our own personal or cultural accounts of what constitutes good and evil. The only moral difference, then, is that one culture finds it horrifying while another culture finds it permissible. This kind of understanding of morality simply devolves into a state of personal preference on par with choosing between two brands of cereal. I choose Trix over Cheerios because I like Trix more than Cheerios. That's pretty much modern ethics in a nutshell. For this reason, the very thing that initially made me a vegetarian, Peter Singer's *Animal Liberation*, was abandoned within a year or two of my reading it. I simply found little recourse in the field of ethics that could function, authoritatively so, to tell me why a person should or should not eat another animal. Since modern ethics locates authority in the very source that once required tutelage (the inner self), I knew I would need to find other sources for couching my understanding of the good and the good that constitutes all of life.[7]

Though I did not give up on my vegetarianism, I did relent on some of the philosophical reasons for it. Personally, I find the means by which cows, chickens, and pigs become food to be horrifying, cruel, vicious, and flat-out immoral. The problem is, I did not think the reasons why I thought such things were enough to convince others that they, too, should think such things. I could only expose the manner in which animals become food in hopes that others would think it was bad too. For some people this may be more than enough. For me, I wanted to ground my vegetarianism in something other than a philosophy of, "But it's so ugly."[8]

After college, I entered a graduate program at Duke University. There I found a number of Christian ethicists and theologians, most of them

7. To give due credit to utilitarians such as Jeremy Bentham and Peter Singer, the one valuable lesson I did learn from them that, unfortunately, I was not quick to locate in theological sources, was the very basic notion that all animals suffer. These philosophers were vital in teaching me that the question does not revolve around whether or not animals think (they do) or have language (they do), but whether or not they suffer (they do). Since animals suffer, and since animals will do whatever they can to avoid pain and suffering, the principal question for anyone attempting to live well with other animals revolves around our own obligations to those beings who can and do suffer.

8. Perhaps a philosophy of "it's so ugly" could be enough. If the Greeks were right that whatever is true must also be good and beautiful, then an ethic of ugliness could be what we need to correct our present abuses of other animals.

omnivores, who were also skeptical of modern philosophical accounts of the good. These were thinkers trying to locate accounts of the good that were authoritative in a way that avoided Enlightenment-based accounts, which placed authority in the recently created entity known as the individual. Rather than looking outside the person in order to be led to the good, modernity inverted this gaze by turning to the subject. The modern philosopher thought that the good was located in the very entity that many premodern philosophers, such as Aristotle, argued was in need of the good. The corrupt agent was now the sole agent of overcoming his corruption. It was this sort of thinking that led many postliberal thinkers to abandon a modern philosophical account of ethics in an attempt to ground knowledge of good and evil in something other than the human will. For my professors at Duke, this meant having conversations within the tradition of Christianity as informed by Greek philosophy and Hebraic thought. For many of these professors, it meant the abandonment of ethics altogether.

This abandonment opens one up to the traditioned resources of cultures such as Judaism and Christianity. The cultures of Judaism and Christianity, along with the influence Greek thought exercised over the latter, offer the kinds of resources that could effect substantial changes to how we understand our environment. These narratives argue a number of very important points that should be welcomed by those in various religious and nonreligious camps.[9] As noted in the previous chapter, the various narratives that constitute Christianity make a number of interesting claims about creation. First, Christianity argues that creation is good, which is no small point (especially when it comes to embodying such a claim). Second, God not only cares for the animals, God makes a number of covenants with all animals (Genesis 9; Hosea 2). Third, and perhaps more importantly for the vegetarian or vegan, humans were initially instructed to not eat animals (Gen 1:29). It is not until after the fall that animal consumption is allowed.[10] Given the eschatological nature of Christianity (to be examined in the next chapter), Christians should be in the business of owning these claims. They should be bearing witness to them. This requires that Christians live in such

9. More than 70 percent of people in the United States claim affiliation with some form of Christianity. Speaking their language, especially for an animal rights advocate who wants to effect change, is not a terribly bad idea.

10. This long-standing account of the so-called fall (read literally or not) has been recently contested by many contemporary biblical scholars. For an interesting book that discusses the problem of animal suffering in light of, and before, the fall, see Osborn's *Death Before the Fall*.

a way that it is clear they believe the claims they make. They must live as if creation is good, as if God has made a covenant with all of creation, as if the violent consumption of other animals is not a part of the original ontological peace God pronounced as good and fitting.

What this looks like will take many different forms. I would never presume to know what such a life would or must look like, only that our claims have to be embodied in such a way that they tell others that we actually believe those claims. This, therefore, does not mean that a Christian must be a vegetarian in order to prove her commitment to these claims; it only means that, on some level, we have to at least experiment with what it may look like to embody these claims. My concern is not so much whether Christians practice vegetarianism, specifically, as much as it is why we tell ourselves it's not an important issue worthy of consideration.[11] I think much of my own understanding as to why I am a vegetarian is far more reliant upon trying to embody these claims as opposed to the simpler and easier-to-understand notion that killing animals for food may be cruel. The Christian narrative, underwritten by an ontology of peace rightly understood only in its eschatological and apocalyptic nature, demands careful attention to how we live with all of creation. That is to say, Christianity's eschatological understanding of time, space, and matter is an integral reason why I am a vegetarian. There are other reasons as well, and despite my unease with stating them, I want to name a few of them now. They may offer a few important insights into how our diets not only affect our thoughts on captivity and conservation but also create the need for certain forms of captivity. Perhaps some of these reasons will serve as a starting point for a discussion of how we understand environmental care, the purpose of animal captivity, and, more importantly, the purpose of other animals.

- I am a vegetarian because I strive to live a life of nonviolence. I know this is not completely possible, because as a white middle-class male living under the protection of the world's strongest superpower I am complicit in many violent activities that make my life possible. I can, nevertheless, abstain from certain forms of violence, and this is one form of violence I can reject.

11. For a detailed analysis of the kinds of questions and considerations Christians have taken in regard to vegetarianism, especially in terms of objections to vegetarianism, see York and Alexis-Baker, *A Faith Embracing All Creatures*.

- I am a vegetarian because I know that cows, chickens, pigs, dogs, cats, armadillos, capuchins, red howlers, red pandas, red foxes, red squirrels, red-tailed hawks, and on and on and on, think, feel, desire, dream, and do whatever they can to seek pleasure and avoid pain. If I can live in such a way as to avoid causing the pain and suffering of animals, then, inasmuch as that is possible, I will do it.

- I am a vegetarian because I *can* be a vegetarian. I live in a part of the world where, nutritionally, I can be as healthy as the healthiest omnivore. Even if I could not be as healthy as the healthiest omnivore, I can be healthy enough to not use it as an excuse to ignore the reality of how my diet affects others.

- I am a vegetarian because I do not believe that animals are commodities that should be marketed according to our personal whims and desires.

- I am a vegetarian because the naming of animals as "meat" does not do justice to the theological purpose of animals.

- I am a vegetarian because any eschatology grounded in the kind of hope that does not overturn our violent natures is not much of an eschatology.

- I am a vegetarian because slaughterhouses offer compelling evidence that humans really are the most brutal species of all. The fact that we mask our brutality by hiding, from ourselves, the very nature and horror of slaughterhouses makes it even worse. We should be above masquerading as *the* civilized species when the truth is that we merely ignore our nightmarish, daily mass killing of other species.

- I am a vegetarian because I do not need more antibiotics in my life (especially those that come secondhand).

- I am a vegetarian because I am opposed to the kind of captivity that reduces an animal's sole purpose to that of becoming human excrement.

- I am a vegetarian because I am against deforestation. To be more specific, I am doing what little I can to resist the destruction of natural habitats that has led to premature animal extinction and the need for many animals to live in zoos and sanctuaries. There *is* a connection.

- I am a vegetarian because I am against starvation. Almost 70 percent of the world's grain goes to feeding animals that feed us. According to

David Pimentel, ecologist at Cornell University, if all of the grain that feeds animals raised for slaughter were, instead, fed to humans, we could easily feed eight hundred million more people a year.[12]

- I am a vegetarian because one kilogram of beef is responsible for more greenhouse gas emissions (and other pollutants) than driving my car for three consecutive hours.[13]

- I am a vegetarian because factory farming accounts for almost 40 percent of methane (CH_4) emissions. Methane has more than twenty times the global warming potential of CO_2.[14]

- I am a vegetarian because the poultry and livestock industries produce more than five hundred million tons of manure a year. (That's some serious shit.) That is far more than can be spread around or considered a healthy amount for the soil. It is, therefore, destroying the soil and finding its way into our water supplies. Enjoy!

- I am a vegetarian because factory farming is destroying our land. It is an ecological disaster, and it robs us of resources that could be shared with those who need them. The continued use of factory farming is short-sighted and will only result in our creating a situation in which we will eventually find ourselves knee-deep in the shit and blood we have spilled in order to eat cheap, desecrated, hormone-injected fast flesh. There is nothing honorable or virtuous about this kind of life. It is disgraceful and represents the embodiment of an embarrassingly shallow theological account of creation.

- I am a vegetarian because, even if all of the above were not true, I would still believe—or, at the very least, I would still hope—that the prophet Isaiah was speaking truthfully when he foretold of the coming peaceable kingdom (Isaiah 11). Part of the reason I continue to be a vegetarian is that I find such hope gives meaning and purpose to what I do, how I live, and what I do and do not eat. In some small way,

12. David Pimentel, along with coauthor Marcia Pimentel, argues that our current consumption of meat, along with our projected population growth over the next half-century, will not only continue to affect the world's starving populations but will have deleterious effects on our own population (as the rate of natural resources required to sustain our diets will far exceed what we can achieve). Pimentel and Pimentel, "Sustainability of Meat-Based and Plant-Based Diets," 660–63.

13. Finelli, "Meat Is Murder on the Environment," 15.

14. Fialla, "How Meat Contributes to Global Warming," 72–75.

I even think that this kind of vegetarianism—one that is premised on this eschatological hope—is a form of practicing resurrection. It bears witness to the original ontological order. It revels in the apocalyptic nature inherent within Christianity. It provides a viable testimony to the kingdom that is coming and the kingdom that is already here.

I hope this last point, if nothing else, creates room for further exploration. It is crucial to any conversation around animal captivity, whether for consumption, entertainment, or conservation, to think about how an eschatological narrative requires us to think differently about any and all forms of captivity. In the following chapter, I will speak more about how eschatology does, or at least might, alter such conversations.

The reasons I have given for my being a vegetarian are by no means exhaustive, nor do I expect them to be entirely persuasive. I did not list them in order to persuade anyone to become a vegetarian. I only listed them in hopes that we could start piecing together certain connections about environmental care and animal captivity. I hope some of my reasons lead us to keep a few important things in mind. First of all, there is a critical connection between how we view animal captivity and our own dietary practices. How we think about animals held in captivity and killed on factory farms is already largely determined by our food selection rather than by any prior thought about the purpose of such places. I do not think we can think well about animal captivity, much less the relationship it has to Christian ethics, if we have not questioned that which makes our meals possible. On this point, we cannot separate the various forms of animal captivity from one another, as our reasons for questioning one and not another say far more about us than animal captivity.

Second, in order to eat animals, at least in the manner made possible via factory farming, we must continue to wage war on our planet and all of its inhabitants. This form of food acquisition is destructive not only to the animals involved but also to our land, our soil, and the countless other animals, human and otherwise, who are directly or indirectly harmed. Simply put, it is just not ecologically sound to continue down this path.

Third, to continue to kill animals for food, especially in slaughterhouses, requires that we ignore or, at the very least, downplay the reality that each animal is a feeling, thinking creature of God who has been deemed good and often suffers a miserable and unimaginably horrid life at our very own hands. Even for those animals who are pasture raised, which is a far superior environment to slaughterhouses, we must still remember that in killing those animals, we are taking the life of a creature who is in a covenant with God and whose sole purpose is directed toward God, not us.

Such thinking, of course, does not mean there is some wholly consistent and perfect manner by which we can reside with other creatures. Even if we make the assumptions above, this does not mean we will find ourselves with the ability to embody an Eden-type vision of the world. This does not, however, let us off of the proverbial hook. In the next chapter, I will examine why our eschatological convictions must be at the forefront of any proper account of biological and covenantal kin. It may be the case that eschatology provides one of the most interesting resources the church has to offer the world. However, in order for it to make sense to the world, it must first make sense to the church. The only way for it to make sense to the church, I contend, is by attempting to embody the present and coming peaceable kingdom. What that looks like is up for debate. Whether or not we do it, however, is not.

INTERLUDE: Growing Mad Farmers

We have lived by the assumption that what was good for us would be good for the world.... We have been wrong. We must change our lives, so that it will be possible to live by the contrary assumption that what is good for the world will be good for us.... For I do not doubt that it is only on the condition of humility and reverence before the world that our species will be able to remain in it.

—WENDELL BERRY, *THE LONG-LEGGED HOUSE*

Fred Bahnson is a good friend of mine. We were graduate students at Duke University, and, since that time, he has become a prominent author, speaker, teacher, and farmer. My claim to fame in connection to Fred's work is that I was the first person to introduce him to the writings of Wendell Berry. Berry had a profound effect on Fred. After Duke, I continued to pursue further graduate work while Fred became a farmer. The work of Berry was important to me, but in a more abstract manner—which is probably the absolute surest way to misread Berry. For Fred, it changed his life. He became involved in various farming projects, was the first director of Anatoth Community Garden in Cedar Grove, North Carolina, and now teaches a variety of courses and seminars on the connection between food and faith. Fred still grows much of his own food and, when possible, kills his own food. It is on this latter point that we have had numerous conversations. I once asked him if he names the animals he kills. He told me he doesn't name the chickens, but he has named some of the hogs. For example, he once had a hog named Chuleta and another named Chorizo (which was just a slick way of saying pork chop and sausage). He told me they "were very, very tasty."

What is so admirable about Fred is his ability to create an alternative to factory farming. His understanding of creation demands that he not participate in a process of unabashed destruction of animals and the environment. For him, ecological stewardship is a necessity. It's not an addendum to Christian living. Probably the one thing we do more than anything else on this planet is eat. Therefore, what we eat, how we eat, and how we obtain our food has to be understood within a rich theology of creation. What I like most about Fred has nothing to do with his books or presentations, but his way of life. It speaks for his understanding of creation.

In an interview I did with him a few years ago, I pressed him on the interconnections between his understanding of creation and eschatology.[1] I wanted to know if his theology of creation included not just the earth but also the earth's inhabitants. I asked him how eschatology drives these connections. I told him I have found that many environmentalists continue to neglect animals in their conversations. It is as if the very beings who exist within and on the land are not part of the environment they find worthy of conserving. I asked him, in relation to a book he cowrote with Norman Wirzba, *Making Peace with the Land: God's Call to Reconcile with Creation*, if he included cows, pigs, and chickens in that reconciliation. Are those creatures a part of God's holy mountain in Isaiah? Are they a part of a redeemed order groaning for completion? If so, *how* are they reconciled with us in any way that actually matters for them in the here and now?

Fred immediately responded with, "Hmm, I detect a vegetarian argument masquerading as a question."

It's true. I've rarely been known for subtlety.

After calling me out, Fred responded, "Yes, animals are included within God's reconciling work. As Colossians 1 tells us, through Christ God has reconciled all things, and that includes animals. But I'm not convinced that we can take metaphorical language in scripture about the New Heaven and New Earth (in Isaiah, for instance) and build an argument about why we should never eat them. The lion may lie down with the lamb *then*, but that doesn't mean the lion can't eat the lamb *now*. At the resurrection, Jesus tells us, 'people will neither marry nor be given in marriage; they will be like the angels in heaven' [Matt 22:30]. But we do marry now, and the church

---

1. Interview with Fred Bahnson, Winter 2013.

blesses that act as a sacrament. I think eating animals can be a sacrament, a sharing of another's life to sustain our own."

After suggesting what appear to be the limits of eschatological realization, he addressed my push toward vegetarianism:

"Too much vegetarianism," he told me, "is ecologically naïve. People think they can avoid the deaths of other creatures. But you can be the strictest vegan and you will still be drawing your nourishment through the deaths of creatures. The farmland that feeds you almost certainly destroyed some creature's habitat. The farmer who grew your pak choi and broccoli most likely had to deal with groundhogs, and here 'deal with' doesn't mean giving them a cuddly head scratch. The truck that rumbled down I-40 from California to bring you the freshest orange at the lowest price ran over countless squirrels, rabbits, deer, and bugs in order to get it to you. And even if you live in a cave and eat bread crusts like St. Anthony, the wheat that made your bread crust grew in soil, and soil thrives on death. If you are a person and you eat food, you are living by the deaths of creatures, whether by your own hand or by proxy. So the responsible thing is, instead of discussing 'whether or not to kill animals,' because we most certainly are killing them, and unavoidably so, is to instead talk about what would make for a *good* death, and what kinds of death are unacceptable. CAFO [Concentrated Animal Feeding Operation] meat is, by any Christian standard, an unacceptable form of death. But to give chickens a pasture to scratch in and eat grass and roll in the dust and frolic in the sun before you eat them? I think you can make a good case that you gave that chicken a good life and a good death. When you end its life to sustain your own life, and you offer up thanks to God for this creature's life, this is not only permissible, it is a sacrament. When you think about it this way, I will say from experience, it becomes very difficult to eat meat often. You don't want that animal's death to be flippantly used or taken for granted. We eat meat once or twice a week, and it's always from animals we either raised or were raised by people we know. Given how little most people know about modern meat production, I think the Christian practice of ascetic denial should become the norm."

Fred's response is nothing if not thought-provoking. In a few words, he offers much to discuss. Unlike many consumers of animal flesh, Fred is not flippant about eating animals. He discusses how his consumption of animals has radically declined due to his sacramental understanding of the kind of sacrifice they must make in order to become food. He denies the good of factory farming, rebels against it with his very own life, and refuses to see this kind of food production as healthy for the environment. He also points out how all of our food comes at a price, and that death is an integral part of what it means to eat, even if we are eating vegetables.

Fred also notes something that most vegetarians and vegans already know: our complicity in ecological violence (or should I say "ecological disorder"?). I'm not sure why "too much vegetarianism" is naïve (and just what *is* too much?), but I think most vegans and vegetarians are well aware that the very presence of humans on this planet entails the death of all kinds of creatures. Indeed, I would argue that most vegetarians understand this more than anyone because it is the exact kind of thing we are always going on and on about. Using that as an argument for killing even more animals, though, strikes me as bizarre and counterintuitive. Just because I inadvertently kill an earthworm or an aphid when I harvest my squash should not condemn me to the kind of attitude that says, "Oh, well. Might as well kill some cows, too." Nevertheless, I am not here to trade blows with my good friend. He's not here to respond and that would not be fair. His comments continue to be helpful because they lead to a number of important questions that, hopefully, will result in a better understanding of why what we eat matters. Such questions include the following:

- How is the eating of animals sacramental? Does that apply to every animal?

- If you give a dog a good life, then can it be sacramental to eat the dog as well? If so, how would we give our dogs a good death? Do we slit their throats or wring their necks?

- What makes one form of killing God-approved and another a horrifying act of cruelty?

- Why does it seem that all dogs go to heaven, but not pigs and chickens? Is each and every one of those animals forgotten by God (Luke 12:6)?

- Does Fred's critique of vegetarianism establish a bad precedent for other nonviolent practices grounded in eschatology, such as Christian pacifism?

- What does it mean to have an eschatology that is grounded in realism?

- If, as Fred says, soil thrives in death, how do we read Gen 1:29, in which all animals are given plants to eat? Is death a natural part of the original good order?

- Since wolves do not currently lie with lambs, should we be expected to show hospitality, mercy, and kindness to other animals?

- Does nature trump eschatology? Is eschatology subservient to any and all of our biological drives?

With many thanks to Fred for allowing me to include our conversation, we now examine what, if anything, eschatology changes in relation to how we understand animal captivity.

6

Can the Wolf Lie Down with the Lamb without Killing It?

Only in art will the lion lie down with the lamb ...

—MARTIN AMIS, *KOBA THE DREAD*

I'm not quite sure whether it was fortuitous or providential, perhaps both, but as I was writing this chapter my spouse, Carly, and I were watching a documentary on wolves. Carly is a doctoral student in the field of ecological science with a fervent commitment to wildlife conservation. So what little time we spend watching television is most often in the company of the Science Channel and National Geographic.[1] It's far more informative than *Two and a Half Men*, and hardly as saccharine. Indeed, as much violence as we have witnessed in the animal kingdom, intra- and interspecies-wise, we had to turn our heads at one particularly vicious moment. The documentary was narrating a territory battle between two

---

1. Animal Planet was, at one time, one of our primary choices in television programming. Over the last few years, however, the channel has radically altered its direction and has opted for shows that exacerbate the notion that most animals primarily seek to cause harm to humans. They have increasingly played up the violent tendencies within a number of species. This occurred, interestingly enough, around the same time that Animal Planet's slogan became "Surprisingly Human."

different families of wolves (wolf packs are typically comprised of blood relatives). As the older pack was forced out by a younger, stronger, and more numerous family of wolves, other creatures in the vicinity had to adapt to the new regime. Two coyotes, a male and a female, who had learned the territorial rules with the previous pack, stumbled upon the new group just as it took over. The wolves quickly descended upon the pair of coyotes. Though the female coyote escaped, her male mate was not so fortunate. At least half a dozen wolves captured the coyote and viciously ripped into its neck, face, and belly, consuming the coyote's entrails while tearing off its face. They showed no mercy; there was no simple nick on the tail given as a warning. The ferocity of the wolves, in light of the coyote's inability to defend itself, was terrifying. As we watched six or seven of them thrash the much smaller coyote, we averted our gaze. We were not surprised so much as we were horrified at the spectacle called "survival."

This is, of course, standard fare in the world. Creatures prey on one another. It is how they survive and provide for their young. What caught us so off-guard was not this reality but its momentary raw brutality. The wolves attacked the coyote not primarily for food, though they did eat him; more than that, the attack was a show of strength, intimidation, and dominance. It was a bloody and violent explanation of the way things were going to be within the territory of this new wolf pack. This was simply their way of asserting themselves so that they could survive. Their behavior was not unforeseen or rare. It's just the way of the world.

As we mourned the loss of the coyote, the female who escaped had to continue living. Though she, too, was in a state of mourning, the next image revealed her in pursuit of a fox. She had immediately changed from prey to predator. In this case, the fox escaped. We were thrilled for the fox. It seemed as if some small victory had occurred in this conflict-torn arena called "nature." Granted, we know that this was probably not much of a victory for the hungry coyote.[2]

The next scene followed the same fox who had just escaped its slightly larger foe. Though we found ourselves hoping the fox would outfox the coyote, our delight at her escape dissipated as she began preying on a number of moles. Though we felt sorrow for the moles caught and consumed,

2. The coyote was, in this case, attempting to kill the fox more for territorial reasons and food scarcity than as a meal. Coyotes are, nevertheless, opportunistic eaters and will certainly eat a fox. For an in-depth examination of the coyote's ability to persevere, especially in light of our perennial efforts to expel it from existence, see De Stefano, *Coyote at the Kitchen Door.*

would we not feel just as much sorrow for a starving fox? What about those creatures who would become food for the moles who escaped becoming food for the fox? The moles escaped their predator only to kill and eat as many invertebrates as they could find. What about *their* lives? Or what about the lives of the smaller invertebrates who fed the larger invertebrates, who fed the moles, who fed the foxes . . . ? At this point, we had no idea who to pull for. In pulling for one individual we were inherently pulling against another, and who are we to determine which creature is of more significance? Do we just base it on the cuteness of the creature? I fear such a response would reveal that we, too, have not escaped the indoctrination of something like *Two and a Half Men*.

Some may be tempted to refer to this cycle of life as vicious and cruel, though many will refer to it as only natural. In the latter sense, it is neither good nor bad. Some naturalists suggest we must simply come to terms with the fact that nature is indifferent to the pain and suffering each creature endures during its brief life. Yet, despite such an outlook, the natural world remains, for some, incredibly beautiful. Whether it is the mountains with their rivers, forests, and abundant "wildlife," or the ocean that hosts incredibly diverse and complex ecosystems in even the shallowest of waters, the planet remains a marvel that boasts of God's goodness and creativity. That such an awareness is often an occasion for arguments for God's existence belies, unfortunately, a very rudimentary and surface-level glance. Such God-ordained beauty often dissipates upon closer examination. The Pisgah Forest in western North Carolina, for instance, is a beautiful landscape teeming with incredible biodiversity. Upon taking a closer look, however, one must consider the vast amount of pain and suffering occurring within it. The forest contains emaciated creatures trying to feed off other emaciated creatures, animals searching for food to give to their offspring (many of whom will not survive infancy), and many other creatures just trying to avoid becoming someone else's meal. Even the trees are in a slow, precarious march to death. As beautiful as the oaks, pines, cedars, and firs may be, they are infested with parasites that can only survive by slowly destroying their scenic hosts. Those parasites are being consumed by other parasites, and those parasites are being destroyed by bacterial parasites. This is called a thriving ecosystem. Nature, we might say in a rather hyperbolic tone, is one big parasite. Even no less a biologist than Charles Darwin remarked,

"What a book a Devil's Chaplain might write on the clumsy, wasteful, blundering low and horridly cruel works of nature."[3]

Perhaps this is a cynical way of approaching nature; then again, perhaps not. Even the biblical writers speak of a time when creation will no longer have to endure the bondage of decay:

> For the creation waits with eager longing for the revealing of the children of God; for the creation was subjected to futility, not of its own will but by the will of the one who subjected it, in hope that creation itself will be set free from its bondage to decay and will obtain the freedom of the glory of the children of God. We know that the whole creation has been groaning in labor pains until now. (Rom 8:19–22)

This is a creation that, while created good, now anxiously awaits its redemption from death, pain, and sorrow. This is especially clear when we juxtapose this reality with the vision of God's holy mountain in Isaiah 11. Despite all of the violence and wastefulness that occurs in nature, Isaiah depicts a time when

> the wolf shall live with the lamb, the leopard shall lie down with the kid, the calf and the lion and the fatling together, and a little child shall lead them. The cow and the bear shall graze, their young shall lie down together; and the lion shall eat straw like the ox. The nursing child shall play over the hole of the asp, and the weaned child shall put its hand on the adder's den. They will not hurt or destroy on all my holy mountain; for the earth will be full of the knowledge of the LORD as the waters cover the sea. (Isa 11:6–9)

While this could be read as a lovely metaphor of how we want things to be, or as a literal interpretation on which Christian hope is predicated, we have to ask certain questions: How practical is this? Can it be lived? Is it not a depiction of a reality completely beyond our control? If this vision is purely impractical, unrealistic, and unlivable, why bother? After all, isn't it the case that carnivores and omnivores require the death of others for their

---

3. How interesting that Darwin referred to nature as cruel. As if, for a naturalist, there can be some point of reference for the meaning of such a word outside of the very thing (nature) he is referencing. Nevertheless, such a quote has been utilized in service of arguments against the existence of God by, in particular, Richard Dawkins; see, for instance, his *Devil's Chaplain*. Such arguments are only persuasive if one has first bought into the idea that God is an agent discoverable in the universe. Surely, orthodoxy protests such a notion, and, ironically, must agree with many of the arguments against the existence of God.

very existence? If so, how realistic is it for Christians to attempt to embody the vision as given in Isaiah? How are we supposed to live in a peaceable-kingdom-world that does not match up with the so-called real world?

A Boy and His (Eschatological) Wolf

For that original goodness that will be one day *all things in all* already shown forth in this saint *all things in all.*

—THOMAS OF CELANO, *ST. FRANCIS OF ASSISI*

The above quote refers to Francis Bernardone, popularly known as St. Francis of Assisi. As is well known, Francis is a patron saint of animals. It would probably be safe to say that he is *the* patron saint of animals (as he is far and away the most famous of a number of them).[4] The quote follows a section in which his first biographer, Brother Thomas of Celano, discusses Francis's interactions with animals. Francis is known for his persistent preaching to any creature who would listen. If all animals belong to God (Ps 24:1), if God cares for all animals (1 John 4:16), if God is concerned with the salvation of animals (Jonah 4:11), and if Jesus commands us to preach to all creation (Mark 16:15), then this means, for Francis, that he too must care for, save, and preach to all creation. He cared for creatures by demanding that we not carelessly wound or hurt any animal, and that we always show compassion for any creature in need. He preached to animals and even demanded that birds and crickets sing songs to their Creator.[5] In one particular case, he even negotiated a tense situation between a wolf and a small community of people. He asked the wolf to cease frightening the people in trade for the very reason the wolf was a so-called problem: food. The hungry wolf was only trying to survive. Due to the fear within the community, a tense situation erupted between the two species, causing constant animosity

4. Francis is also the patron saint of the environment. I have never understood the separation of animals, human or nonhuman, from something called "the environment." For more literature on various saints and animals, see Waddell's *Beasts and Saints*. Despite its unfortunate name, the book includes a number of interactions between Christianity's most devout and various individuals from the animal kingdom. It also contains beautiful images of woodcuts by Robert Gibbings.

5. Thomas, *St. Francis of Assisi*, 269–74. For more on how Francis understood all creation in terms of salvation, see my chapter "Christianity Is for the Birds" in York, *Third Way Allegiance*, 25–27.

THE END OF CAPTIVITY?

and anxiety. Francis negotiated between the two, discovered the root of the problem, and created a solution. After asking both parties to repent of their sins, he commanded the wolf to cease terrorizing the people, as they are made in the image of God, and the people to do their part—practice hospitality to the stranger. This arrangement worked for several years, with the wolf going door to door for food and with each person caring for the creature, until the wolf died. By this time, the small community had grown attached to the wolf and lamented the wolf's death.

Though this story may very well be the product of exaggeration, what is significant is that Francis's biographers viewed him as the paradigmatic example of how to deal with human-wildlife conflict. Though there is now an abundance of PhD programs rooted in this very discipline, for most of human history resolution has often meant the killing of the nonhuman.[6] This is important because Francis's sainthood is interwoven with his understanding of how all creation participates in the salvific economy of the triune God. Creation is not inconsequential to salvation. If matter does not matter then salvation, the redemption of all flesh, is meaningless. Because the medieval church was very well guarded against Gnosticism—specifically its refusal to see creation as a direct good from God with its concomitant desire to seek salvation from the material world—it at least had the resources to understand that redemption is not something meant for intangible souls. The redemption of creation is material, and includes all creation. If salvation is not deliverance of the very "thing" God pronounced good, then we might as well eat, drink, and be merry, for tomorrow we die.

---

6. However, medieval law applied to animals and humans in which serious trials and lawsuits were argued with canon lawyers appointed to argue on behalf of the animals and on the prosecution side. These trials were expensive, time-consuming affairs that showed just how seriously they were taken. Sometimes the animals won. For example, a French jurist named Bartholomé Chassenée (1480–1542) successfully defended a community of rats against a lawsuit by arguing that the rats failed to appear in court because they had been threatened by too many cats! And when an ecclesial court excommunicated field mice in Glurns for destroying crops in 1520, the court also granted a pardon to all pregnant and adolescent mice. Thus communication between humans and animals was not solely the province of exceptional saints or superstitious peasants, but educated, serious people as well. Even great Enlightenment thinkers like Gottfried Wilhelm Leibniz wrote about animal trials in all seriousness (see Leibniz, *Theodicy*, 1:314). In this way, nonhuman animals were placed within the community of justice and not outside of it as they are in our modern, rationalized technological society. For more on this, see Dinzelbacher, "Animal Trials," 405–21, as well as Jeffrey St. Clair, "Let Us Praise Infamous Animals," in Hribal, *Fear of the Animal Planet*, 1–8. I am grateful to Andy Alexis-Baker for reminding me of this much-neglected aspect of medieval history.

I introduce Francis into this chapter because he disrupts the poverty of our imaginations. He does so by thinking it crucial, for faithful Christian existence, to live a resurrected life in light of Christianity's eschatological nature. His life is a crowning example of what it means to live in a particular kind of world that only some people can see. Christianity (as with any religion or culture) provides a particular lens for how its adherents can navigate the world. A vital part of Christianity's lens, or grammatical framework, revolves around time—specifically, there being a beginning, middle, and an end. Christianity asserts that, prior to the primordial fall, creation was at peace with itself. How such peace was originally undone is something of a mystery, but many within Christianity have suggested that it was undone through human disobedience, and this placed creation at odds with its creator.[7] This, too, was an act of creation. It created the secular, not as a domain but as a time. The secular is the time between times, rife with violence, sickness, death, war, famine, and destruction. Once this time is no more, the end will resemble the beginning inasmuch as all will be subsumed into its original purpose.

This particular manner in which Christians see the world renders Christianity eschatological. Christian faith is, as James McClendon argues, an inherently eschatological faith:

> It sees the present in correct perspective only when it construes the present by means of the prefiguring past (God's past) while at the same time construing it by means of the prophetic future (God's future). "This is that" declares the present relevance of what God has previously done, while "then is now" does not abolish the future but declares the present relevance of what God will assuredly do.[8]

McClendon is arguing that inasmuch as Christianity is eschatological, it refuses any sort of depiction of the world as "that's just the way it is." By its very eschatological nature, Christianity resists the inherent violence assumed in accounts of nature that tempt us to imagine death as a prerequisite to life,

---

7. Such an understanding of the "fall" is problematic for a number of reasons. First, it does not accurately reflect what is going on in the text. The serpent is already at odds with the purpose of creation prior to the story of Adam and Eve. Also, scientific evidence reveals a violent world prior to the introduction of humans—that is, the Tyrannosaurus rex was not a vegetarian. How the fall could ever occur is a more interesting theological debacle. For a discussion of the impossibility of the fall, see Milbank, *Being Reconciled*, 1–25.

8. McClendon, *Doctrine*, 69.

and it protests the sort of pragmatic realism that tempts Christians to lead lives of practical atheism. What this demands is to properly understand creation's purpose—which, Christianity claims, is to glorify the triune God. All of creation, from the red howler monkey to the Indonesian mimic octopi, exists to glorify God. Of course, there is very little to suggest that these creatures recognize this as their purpose, as they are, along with humans, doing everything they can just to survive.[9] Nevertheless, one of the central claims of Christianity is that creation is ongoing, and that it is, ultimately, a narrative of fulfillment. Stanley Hauerwas and John Berkman argue that it is from "our conviction that God redeems all of creation we learn that God, having created all things, wills that all things enjoy their status as God's creatures."[10] A Christian account of creation, therefore, does not end with the first two chapters of Genesis but must include passages such as Romans 8 and Isaiah 11. Creation can be properly understood only in light of its original purpose, its ongoing struggle with fulfilling that purpose, and its ultimate completion. This is why the witness of someone like St. Francis is so vital to how Christianity tells its own story. Francis's very life was a gospel. By that I mean that it was good news to all creatures because he attempted to reflect the gospel that is Jesus for all of creation—not just one species. He understood that all animals, insomuch as they have a common creator, were both his covenant partners and his kin (and this is centuries prior to Darwin!). What led Francis to avoid stepping on worms, for example, or to set out food for insects in the winter was not that he was an "obsessed animal lover" but that he understood the purpose/end of creation. Because he lived an eschatological life, he could not imagine behaving otherwise toward that which God declares "good." Francis imagined that humans were in the privileged position to name and care for all animals in the manner in which Jesus names and cares for all of us. This meant that he was able to resist seeing animals as mere objects for our own use.

It is precisely on this point that Christians name other animals well when they are named eschatologically. In order to do this faithfully, we have to be able to name animals in such a way that our treatment of these creatures tells them, and others, who we think they are in light of the purpose of creation. This is no easy task, as the principalities and powers have tempted

9. Most creatures, if not all, need to survive only long enough to reproduce—which is what many biologists and zoologists will say is a creature's only real (or at least empirical) purpose.

10. Hauerwas and Berkman, "Trinitarian Theology of the 'Chief End,'" 69.

many of us to forfeit any rich eschatological understanding of our own narrative. For instance, because we imagine that pigs should be named "bacon," or snakes "belts," or crocodiles "boots," or elephants "circus entertainment," or cows "milk machines," or rabbits "safe cosmetics," the difficulty lies in the recovery of adequate theological language. Is it not the case that the story of creation, as found in Genesis, Isaiah, and Romans, provides us with resources for giving animals names other than these?

If so, I imagine the first eschatological act we must perform, as intimated above, is getting our language right. If we are to be faithful to our own narrative, then the naming of animals must correlate with our habits and practices as informed by God's peaceable kingdom. If Christians and non-Christians are to see a world that is intelligible in light of our claims, then we must speak, and perform, a very particular kind of language. For instance, as a thought experiment, what if we ceased using descriptions that label animals as products, cosmetics, food, clothing, entertainment, and pets[11] and decided to call them, first and foremost, *our covenant partners*? Wouldn't that be profoundly more biblical than the previous alternatives? What difference, if any, would that make? Or what if we resisted the story that the biomedical sciences have imposed upon us and renamed "lab rats" our "kin"? How could a Christian ever faithfully call a creature of God a lab rat? From what story does that originate? Is that a label to be applied by those who think that God created, ordered, and redeemed the world, or is that a description of a world in rebellion against that which God called good?

So, instead of calling animals food, cosmetics, medicine, clothing, and entertainment, we should begin to refer to them as manifestations of God's creative wisdom who are our covenant partners participating in God's redemptive history. This does not romanticize nature or the animal kingdom; it simply names the world biblically, eschewing the common misconception that animals exist for no other reason than for our species-centric benefit. What are Christians saying about creation's purpose when we name it based on how only one species may plunder its goods for whatever uses our greed leads us to invent? Is this not a poor witness to the way the world was created, was meant to be, and will, one day, be again? Is it not both our burden and privilege to embody Isaiah's vision so that others may catch a

---

11. Stephen Webb offers the most persuasive argument I have encountered for retaining the word *pet*. I remain, however, unconvinced that such language can fully bring about the kind of mutuality Webb desires. For a thorough discussion on the use of this language, see his *On God and Dogs*, 69–84.

glimpse of that which we claim to be true? While it is true that the kingdom is not yet fully realized, it is up to Christians to be faithful to their understanding of creation, so that others will know there is an alternative to this vision of a world at war with itself. Otherwise, how can anyone know that there is a different way of interpreting creation, one unlike what appear to be the senseless, wasteful, and cruel practices of the cold and indifferent cycle called nature?[12]

A Boy and His (Eschatological) Crocodile

It is we who have to change, not they.... If Virgil and Beatrice have to change according to someone else's standards, they might as well give up and be extinct.

—YANN MARTEL, *BEATRICE AND VIRGIL*

On September 4th, 2006, Steve Irwin, also known as the "Crocodile Hunter," was killed by a stingray.[13] Although many of his admirers and critics had expressed concern about the risk of his hands-on approach with creatures, his death still came as a shock. Perhaps part of the shock stems from our celebrity-obsessed culture's tendency to attach immortality to celebrities. While I think this may be partly true, I think it may have had more to do with the manner in which he was killed: impaled through the chest by a nonaggressive creature that has claimed the lives of only a handful of people in Australian waters. Indeed, stingrays are sort of the "petting-zoo" creature of the waters. There is even a tank where you can touch and feed stingrays in the Opry Mills Outlet Mall in Nashville, Tennessee (as well as

12. I am not suggesting that only Christians can provide this alternative. If this were the case, I fear that the world would be without much hope at all! Clearly, other religions, cultures, and naturalists produce groups and individuals that embody an alternative to our participation in an assumed ontologically ridden violent world. Indeed, it appears that naturalists with little to no religious affiliation are out-narrating Christians on their own accounts of creation. (Many thanks to Melanie Kampen, who also reminded me it is imperative to listen to other Christian and non-Christian traditions outside of Western thought. We often think our Western understandings of nature are somehow inherent to Christianity and the Bible. This needs to be continually challenged.)

13. This latter section draws heavily from a previously published article of mine titled "Crocodile Lover: Learning from Steve Irwin," 9–10. It was also republished with the title "The Theological Significance of One Strange Australian" in York, *Third Way Allegiance*, 28–32.

in countless aquariums). That Irwin was killed by such a passive creature is surely ironic and difficult to believe.[14]

On this point, I find Irwin's life to be of significance for Christian reflection. His life was, in many ways (intentionally or not), an eschatological witness to the way the world was created, its intention and purpose, and to the manner in which it will be redeemed. He did not treat nonhuman animals as many animal rights advocates wish them to be treated: leave them to their own devices. He did not think it was responsible to bow to the complaints of groups like PETA that wanted him to stop touching nonhuman animals and interfering with their lives. As we already know, it's way too late for that. We have already touched them and interfered with their lives—and in the most damaging ways. Irwin acknowledged criticisms of his approach, yet he argued that if there is any hope for animal conservation then we have to be as physically involved as possible.[15] He took, I believe, a more biblical approach in that he recognized nonhuman animals as our kin. He did not simply let creatures be; rather, he intervened on their behalf because he recognized the beauty, the goodness, and the mystery that is found within all of creation. He saw these animals as fellow creatures who desperately require our care. As with Francis, he understood that there was a commonality that linked all creatures, regardless of species. Neither Irwin nor Francis was able to understand how anyone could be indifferent

14. In an interview, popular conservationist Jack Hanna said of Irwin's death, "I never pictured a croc doing it, but I never pictured a stingray doing it, either. It's like me being killed by a poodle." See http://usatoday30.usatoday.com/news/world/2006-09-04-obit-irwin_x.htm.

15. There is legitimacy to many of the complaints against Irwin's approach to conservation. Chasing, grabbing, and jumping on animals certainly causes undue stress to each individual. It can also, unwittingly, teach others that this is the appropriate way to handle animals (if they should be handled at all). Irwin argued that proper handling, especially in a land like Australia (where everything seems to be poisonous and venomous), is important in terms of knowing how to negotiate human-nonhuman conflict. He also found it important in terms of teaching people how to love that which they might otherwise deem unlovable. He would often say that people want to save that which they love, and so he wanted to present as intimate a picture of animals as possible. Prior to his becoming an international success, there were a couple of ongoing television shows preaching the importance of animal conservation. There are now more than thirty. I find that to be a far more compelling and successful approach than throwing fake blood on people wearing fur (as tempting as that may be). Nevertheless, for a helpful conversation arguing for and against celebrity conservationists, their tactics, and how Irwin was not always consistent in regard to understanding a number of ecological issues in his homeland, see Paquette, "Importance of the 'Crocodile Hunter' Phenomenon," and Bradshaw et al., "Dangers of Sensationalizing Conservation Biology."

to the plight of creation. For either creation is good or it is not good—and if it is good, then it cannot be good for that which God called good to be destroyed.

At the same time, I want to be careful not to underwrite any kind of mawkish idealism. Irwin never romanticized wildlife, and neither should we. He never imagined that if one simply spent enough time caring for a crocodile that it would become his friend.[16] That was, of course, neither his task nor his calling. His job was to help spread the good word of wildlife conservation. Though acting on their behalf, he never assumed that such creatures would ever thank or love him for it. Yet, this is what makes his witness all the more interesting. His love for these creatures is all the more impressive since it was, generally speaking, non-reciprocal. He did not love a creature because of the possibility of a mutual love affair; rather, he loved these creatures simply because they were creatures. He loved them because they reflect creation's mystery. He loved them because he loved the world. He called snakes, crocs, spiders, and many other dangerous creatures "beauts." That is, I imagine, part of what it means to name creatures well. He looked at animals with an entirely different lens than that which many of us are accustomed to wearing. Despite creation's present parasitical nature, despite those things we might see as wasteful, cruel, or ugly, he was able to see something much deeper. He practiced a vision of how things could or should be, and for that, he lived a kind of incarnational theology that puts many of us to shame.

16. At his memorial service, Steve's father, Bob Irwin, said, "Please do not grieve for Steve, he's at peace now. Grieve for the animals. They have lost the best friend they ever had, and so have I." I take this as recognition that Steve was the best advocate a crocodile, Komodo dragon, banded sea snake, or any other animal, for that matter, could find. Of course, some animal advocates would disagree. See, for instance, Hribal, *Fear of the Animal Planet*. Hribal protests, in particular, the kind of animal handling found in circuses and zoos. While this book is an indispensable collection of stories displaying various animals' refusal to act according to human desires, it is, unfortunately, egregiously unsophisticated in its understanding of both animal behavior and the work of zoos. Every example used to buttress Hribal's case actually finds agreement with the very people (zookeepers in particular) he thinks he is condemning. It's part of the reason why AZA-accredited zoos are altering their purpose to focus primarily on conservation, habitat rehabilitation, and breeding and release programs. Much of animal keeping is moving to a protected or no-contact policy that, unfortunately, has to continue displaying animals that cannot be re-released into the wild so that these conservation centers can help ensure that other creatures will not need to end up in zoos. As stated in the first two chapters, many zoos, conservation centers, and wildlife parks actually function as a safe place *from* humans. If anything, that is certainly a stronger condemnation of human-animal interactions than that of the relatively minute number of careless animal keepers.

Many times, as I watched the *Crocodile Hunter Diaries*, I would reflect on Isa 11:6: "The wolf shall live with the lamb, the leopard shall lie down with the kid, the calf and the lion and the fatling together, and a little child shall lead them." When one watched the crocodile hunter in action, it was easy to compare him to the kind of child referenced in Isaiah. He never seemed to see a world that most "responsible" people demand we embody; instead, he looked upon creation with the eyes of a child—one that could play over the "hole of the asp" and put his "hand on the adder's den" (Isa 11:8).[17]

Nevertheless, Steve Irwin was killed by one of the very creatures he loved so dearly. The fact that a stingray plunged its spine into his chest while he was filming a documentary on the deadliest creatures in the ocean should not be lost on us. We live in a world at odds with itself, and no one understood this better than Irwin. Creation awaits redemption, and it is only in light of this redemption that we can appropriately understand something called "creation." We pine for that moment when "nothing harmful will take place on the LORD's holy mountain" (Isa 11:9), but until then, all we have are glimpses of God's peaceable kingdom. A few saints and a handful of popular conservationists such as Steve Irwin, Jane Goodall, Jeff Corwin, Richard O'Barry, and Jean-Michel and Philippe Cousteau provide us with such a glimpse. Though these conservationists differ radically in their approach (and it is in their differences that I think we have the best

17. Irwin was not a vegetarian. Given his harsh comments about Australians' eating kangaroos and other cultures consuming snakes or dolphins, it's hypocritical that he ate cows. Were they not "beauts"? Irwin considered being a vegetarian but thought it better for a larger body of wildlife that he eat some flesh. He said, "I went through a big stage of my life where I thought, you know, maybe it would be better to be a vegetarian, so I researched it. In no uncertain terms did I research it. Let's say this represents one cow, which will keep me in food for, let's say, a month. Now that cow needs this much land and food. Well, you can imagine, that cow needs x by x amount of land, and you can grow trees in it. Around that cow, you can have goannas, kangaroos, wallabies. You can have every other single Australian animal in and around that cow. If I was a vegetarian, to feed me for that month, I need this much land, and nothing else can grow there. Herein lies our problem. If we level that much land to grow rice and whatever, then no other animal could live there except for some insect pest species. Which is very unfortunate." Interview with Steve Irwin, *Scientific American*, March 26, 2001, http://www.scientificamerican.com/article.cfm?id=part-2-protecting-wildlif. What is most unfortunate is his incredibly naïve understanding of how atrocious breeding cattle for food is for the environment. Also, cows, too, must eat. They require a whole lot of land, as Irwin argued, in which nothing else can grow. His defense is just baffling. The amount of land required to grow food for vegetarians/vegans is a fraction of what is required to breed and sustain animals for our consumption.

chance for improving our approach at habitat and species conservation), they provide us with an intelligible means of participating in this ongoing narrative called creation. In this time between times, they are curiously faithful practitioners of the eschatological vision we find in Isaiah. I say "curiously" because, in the case of the abovementioned conservationists, it is by no means clear that any of these people utilize biblical resources for doing what they do. In this sense, as in so many others, Christians are being out-narrated by individuals who seem to have a more faithful understanding of what it means to live peaceably than those within our own tradition.[18] It is the experimental witness of such people that provides hope that there is some alternative to simply biding our time, waiting for an intervention, and just embodying the fallen nature of this world. It's simply not enough for us to say, "Well, wolves eat lambs, therefore I can too." To be ensnared in such an argument is to concede our most important resource for that which we claim to be true: our witness. The point is not what are we going to do to keep the wolf from killing the lamb, but how are we going to live lives that reflect our tradition's best claims as to the *purpose* of all creation. Doesn't the refusal to eat or wear animal flesh point to this ordained end? Or what about those people who dedicate their lives to healing sick creatures, caring for them, binding their wounds and raising the orphaned so that they can live lives that reflect the beauty and mystery of creation? Is this not a witness to that for which we were created? If ours is a faith that is eschatological in nature, what are we waiting for? To be sure, it may be the case that what we, undoubtedly, are waiting for (to paraphrase a famous philosopher) is another—doubtless very different—St. Francis . . . or, Steve Irwin.[19]

18. This should not, for two reasons, be interpreted as an argument for anonymous Christianity. First, I wish to avoid such imperialism, and second, this would assume that there is something in Christianity for these people to gain in their approach to animal conservation. I'm not sure, at least within the parameters of North American contemporary Christianity, there is anything for anyone outside of Christianity to learn that would be beneficial to animal conservation. Christians are the ones who need to be on the learning side of what it might mean to envision the wolf lying down with the lamb, and it starts by studying the lives of the aforementioned conservationists as well as reading the works of, to name just a few, Frans de Waal, J. Moussaieff Masson, Marc Bekoff, Sue Coe, Mark Rowlands, Amy Hatkoff, Cleveland Amory, and Ruby Roth.

19. I am indebted to Claire Priddy and Carly Anne York for their invaluable suggestions on an earlier draft of this chapter.

INTERLUDE: Not Enough Buckets

I live a ridiculously privileged life. At any given moment on any given day, I get to do what brings me peace and contentment, and brings a big fat smile to my face: I get to surf. Surfing, when it's just right, has almost made a Taoist out of me. I say "almost" only because I don't really know what it means to be a Taoist. I've taught Taoism in world religions courses, and I have a few friends who claim it as their lifestyle, but I don't really see that much difference between how they live and how the Christian fundamentalist next door to me lives. I think they vote differently, and both groups get very angry about their voting differences, but that's about it. All I know is, there is nothing I enjoy more than simply letting go of the fight and riding one of the earth's most powerful forces. This is what Taoists call wu-wei. Often translated as "nonaction," wu-wei refers to just letting go, or simply going where nature takes you. Despite the occasionally brutal riptide (or upwelling that can create, overnight, a twenty-degree drop in water temperature), surfing—that letting go (or going with)—brings me an incredible sense of peace. It allows me to get my peace on. And to call forth the late John Lennon, isn't that what we're all trying to do?

Last summer I was walking across the rather hot sands of the northern Outer Banks beaches on my way to a secluded surf spot by Duck Pier when this kid who was fishing started freaking out. He had accidentally caught a stingray. He was upset, it seemed, not because he had caught something so beautiful and borderline surreal, but rather because he had no idea how to get it off his line. He admitted that he was scared to go anywhere near it. After all, a stingray killed an animal handler no less experienced than Steve Irwin, so he wasn't going to touch it. I told him not to panic. I explained to him that stingrays are generally very docile and are only a threat to humans when threatened—which, of course, was this particular moment.

Since stingrays obviously need to be in the ocean to survive, I was moving as quickly as possible. I gently placed my surfboard on the sand and intervened as if I were a trained marine biologist. I grabbed the pectoral fins and flipped him over on his back (which keeps that lovely serrated spine of his from being an issue of concern). The mouth of the stingray is on its belly—perfect placement for creatures who enjoy eating on the seabed. Since a stingray has teeth I didn't want to stick my fingers in its mouth in order to retrieve the rather large brass hook connected to the fishing line. Fortunately, another fisherman stepped in with some pliers and was able to get the hook out of his mouth. We then flipped him back over and proceeded to direct the ray back in the water. A few onlookers asked if we would wait, as they wanted to take pictures. I stepped back long enough for a few pictures to be taken then quickly suggested we get it back in the water. We positioned the ray back in the ocean and he slowly disappeared. Numerous people cheered as if we had just saved a large marine mammal (stranded dolphins are a real crowd-pleaser around here). The group that had gathered was sending all of their pictures to their friends and families. They were asking lots of questions about its feeding habits, its potential threat to humans, and how, to quote Marvin Gaye, they "get it on." While trying to respond with the most accurate answers an amateur marine biologist like me can provide, I was impressed by how most of the people saw the ray as a beautiful manifestation of God's wisdom and creativity. Granted, one lady did ask how I found it possible to get in the water knowing that stingrays, sharks, and jellyfish share that space. I told her I didn't really think about it. This is, after all, their home, and nine times out of ten most ocean-dwelling creatures—save for, perhaps, the rather grumpy bull shark—are going to do everything they can to avoid contact with us. To be honest, that seems to be the one thing they have in common with land animals: avoid humans.

To be sure, every jellyfish sting, as well as every cut I've received from the cheliped of a blue crab (or some other crustacean), has originated from me making contact with them. I've never been "attacked" by anything in the ocean, and I hope and pray—especially whenever I see a dorsal fin popping out of the water—that it stays that way.

What was most interesting to me was the response of the onlookers. As I said, they were discussing its beauty, its fantastic features, and many people were appreciative that we went out of our way to save it. This relatively short brush with an elusive stingray had inspired awe and wonder in those fortunate enough to see it. As the stingray made its way back into the water, however, someone did mention that stingrays are edible. "They make for a meaty meal," claimed a tourist with his requisite OBX t-shirt. Another man, who had just caught a croaker, protested that making a meal of the stingray would be cruel. Why it was not cruel to the individual fish suffocating on the end of his line was not clear to me. Croakers are surely beautiful in their own right, and they make these interesting repetitive sounds that are best described as, well, croaking. Given that I was on my way to enjoy a rather decent-sized and clean swell, I was in no mood to open up that, forgive the expression, "can of worms." We had saved a stingray and educated a few people on the anatomy and habits of this incredible creature. It was a good day. I felt like Jacques Cousteau. A hero to all marine life.

As I continued my trek to the pier, I noticed the tide going out. A few yards in front of me, not more than fifty feet from the rescued stingray, was a little girl, approximately seven or eight years of age, playing in a small puddle that the disappearing tide had created. She was shoveling something in a bucket, sprinting to the ocean, and then emptying the bucket into the ocean. I realized she was transferring tiny fish (most likely the bay anchovy) from the puddles to the ocean. Due to the lack of oxygen in these small pockets of water, the fish were suffocating. The young girl was frantically doing all she could to save what must have been thousands of these creatures. She was on the verge of tears, as neither time nor the size of her bucket was on her side. I asked her if she had any friends who could help and she shook her head, emphatically telling me "no." I, once again, put my surfboard down, grabbed her bucket and helped transfer as many fish back into the ocean as possible. We couldn't save them all, but we did save probably forty or fifty of them. By the time we finished emptying the puddle of all the remaining live fish, I looked toward the north end of the beach and noticed thirty to forty more of these same puddles—all inescapable death traps for these tiny fish. The little girl was oblivious to the plight of the others and I certainly didn't feel inspired to tell her about them. At best, she could have saved only a small percentage anyway, and I wanted her to feel as if she had really accomplished something. I didn't want her to become a cynic at such a young age. That development must be reserved for her late twenties.

As I looked back at the dispersing crowd, I wondered why none of them were interested in taking pictures of this little Jane Goodall of the fish world. She had saved many more lives than I, so why was she of no interest to the beachgoers? Rather than grow distrustful of the tourists' lack of interest, I instead reflected on the small glimmer of hope this girl represented. Here was a child unspoiled by the cultural indoctrination that only measures animals through the species-centric lens of human use. While every other brat on the beach (is that a song by the Ramones?) was whining about the weather being too hot, or the water being too cold, or their rich parents' failure to stop the waves from crushing their uninspired sandcastles, this little girl had somehow found it within herself to shed tears for dying fish. I could only conclude that a divine intervention had taken place in the rearing of this child.

As I made my way to my favorite surf spot, feeling rather self-satisfied by my good deeds of the day, I tried not to pay any attention to the thousands upon thousands of fish stranded on the beach. I could not, however, avoid noticing a large mass of jellyfish and sponges awash on the shore. High tide had been rather cruel. But I was not to be bothered. I had waves to catch and peace to find. I wanted to contemplate the Tao as I rode down the line of chest-high waves. I wanted to float on my board while staring at a pod of dolphins jumping in and out of the same waves I was surfing. I wanted to reflect on the strained juxtaposition of natural selection with God's purpose for creation. I wanted to ignore the absurd splendor of a billion little ecosystems home to so much pain and suffering. I wanted to feel the earth move me in such a way that I was above the complex systems of life and death cycling under the immediate surface of the waves. After all, the water was warm, the sets were consistent, and the dolphins were playing.

A few hundred yards back the little girl had discovered the other puddles of dying fish. She was frantically filling her bucket as the rest of us blissfully enjoyed the warm waters of the Atlantic Ocean.

EPILOGUE: Searching for Hanno

The Indian elephant is said sometimes to weep.

—CHARLES DARWIN, *THE EXPRESSIONS OF THE EMOTIONS IN MAN AND ANIMALS*

It was a frigid Saturday morning and I was happy to be inside the elephant barn. During the winter we keep the barn nice and cozy for the elephants. I was warming up prior to heading outside to shovel the incredible amount of poop deposited overnight by the bongos. Just as I was about to go outside, someone behind me thought it would be funny to spray me down. For a brief moment, I thought one of the keepers had inadvertently (or not) drenched me with a hose. Given the temperature outside, I was not prepared to find it humorous. When I turned to locate the culprit, I recognized that the guilty party was a member of the species *Loxodonta africana*: the African elephant. In particular, it was the forty-year-old matriarch, Lisa. Apparently, upon walking into the barn, I had neglected to pay respectful attention to her. She quickly informed me of my sin by filling her trunk with water and spraying me. It was her way of letting me know that when I walk into her barn, it would be prudent to recognize her existence. By ignoring her, I was snubbing her position as top mammal in the building.[1]

1. The Virginia Zoo, like almost all AZA-accredited zoos, works under protected contact. Protected contact means there are barriers that separate humans from elephants and that working with the elephants requires much less physical contact than previous policies under free contact.

While I admit it is a pretty awesome experience to be hosed down by an elephant, I was not looking forward to going outside in wet clothes. I think she somehow knew it would make me uncomfortable because she never once sprayed me during the summer. I would have welcomed it on those hot days. Instead, she soaked me on one of the coldest mornings I can remember. Kudos to her because, from then on, I made sure I said hello to her every single time I walked into the barn.

Of all the animals I've had the good fortune to be around, elephants are one of the few species I always felt constantly evaluating me. That's not to say that other animals do not evaluate us, as I'm convinced they do, it's just that every time I looked into the eyes of an elephant I experienced the overwhelming sense that I was being analyzed and judged. Sometimes it was clear that they were just looking at me to see if I had any treats, while at other times it was obvious that something else was occurring. These highly complex and social creatures, with their big brains and long memories, were thinking about me as I was thinking about them. To watch another animal think about you as they look at you, as is obviously evident in so many species, is a humbling thing. I suddenly became aware not so much of my thoughts about them as much as their thoughts about me. I don't mean this in the sense that I could tell what they were thinking; rather, it hit me that what was important might not be so much what I think about them as much as what they think about me. Granted, I assume much of what they think about me is based on what I think about them (and how I show such thoughts), and so our thoughts are, to some degree, reciprocally constitutive. Every elephant caregiver from circuses to zoos to sanctuaries will tell you over and over again that it is all about building relationships with elephants. I believe them when they tell me this because I have seen these relationships in action. While everything I have ever witnessed has been extremely positive (I've only ever witnessed tactics of positive reinforcement, never any form of punishment), many of these relationships, historically speaking, have been one-sided. A quick perusal of elephant and human relationships in North America reveals relationships predicated upon fear, violence, punishment, and dominance. Elephants in the United States have been beaten into submission, chained, whipped, punched, shot, electrocuted, and even lynched.[2] Fortunately, many of those days are now in the past. It is highly unlikely we will ever see another public execution

2. For more information on some of the horrid deaths that elephants have faced—in particular, the lynching of the elephant Mary—see Davis, *The Circus Age*; Tobias, *Behemoth*; Brant, *Elephant's Graveyard*; and Price, *The Day They Hung the Elephant*.

of an elephant and, at least in terms of accredited zoos, the ankus (bull-hook) has been all but stripped from the keeper. Of course, these negative relationships only attest to part of the story. While there is no shortage of stories of bad handlers and the elephants who retaliated, there is also no shortages of stories of elephants bonding with their human companions.[3] I have witnessed firsthand humans and elephants caring for one another in such a manner that it could easily be defined as reciprocated love. Asking if this is natural or ideal may not matter to the two animals, human and elephant, who have bonded. Humans and elephants, and countless other species, have the ability to love and bond with animals outside of their species. They do so under all sorts of conditions, ideal or not.

Placing the convoluted issue of human and elephant relationship aside, what is of utmost importance is addressing the individual needs of captive animals. By individual needs, I am not simply talking about food, shelter, and veterinary care. Those should be givens. If you are holding animals captive, for whatever reason, providing them with the basic necessities of life should be a given. What I am addressing here, in terms of needs, is how we can ensure that captive animals find comfort, ease, and enjoyment in their captivity. As Jeffrey Masson asks, what can we do to make them happy? What can we do to enable them to flourish?[4] Many scientists, biologists, and zoo officials are not interested in discussing "flourishing" and "happiness." They often find such language to be anthropomorphic.[5] While I agree that humans should not project their own needs and desires onto

3. The documentary *One Lucky Elephant* is a very compelling one, if for no other reason than a circus producer (David Balding) wishes to retire his elephant (Flora) in order to provide her with a better home. Throughout the documentary, however, it is never quite clear that her separation from David is a good thing. While David understands that he cannot provide her with a home that meets her needs, Flora's attachment to David is abundantly evident. Flora eventually finds a home at the Elephant Sanctuary in Hohenwald, Tennessee. Carol Buckley, who cofounded the sanctuary, was actually part of the early training sessions that made it possible for Flora to become a circus elephant (Carol, too, once worked in circuses). Carol subsequently denied David visitation rights to Flora. In 2010, Carol was dismissed from the sanctuary and, in what is perhaps a rather karmic act, has been denied visitation rights to her own elephant, Tarra. For more information on Flora, see http://www.elephants.com/flora/floraBio.php; for more on Carol Buckley and Tarra, see http://www.carolbuckley.com/tarra.php. See also the documentary's website: http://www.oneluckyelephant.com/.

4. Masson and McCarthy, *When Elephants Weep*, 99–101.

5. For a defense of a certain kind of anthropomorphism, see Masson and McCarthy, *When Elephants Weep*; Midgley, *Animals and Why They Matter*; and Bekoff, *Why Dogs Hump and Bees Get Depressed*.

other animals, I disagree with the blanket condemnation inherent within the constant and oversimplified protest against anthropomorphism. Until biologists and behaviorists can prove that animals do not have emotions, we must take those emotions into consideration when keeping animals captive. Of course, I do not know of a single caregiver who would deny that animals have emotions; I'm just not sure they are always allowed to act as if those emotions should determine their overall care. For example, when people ask questions like, "Why does that elephant look so sad?" we must resist the temptation to fall back on the preprogrammed response, "Don't be anthropomorphic." Instead, we need to seek to find out what sort of conditions we can create to bring that elephant the most joy. It very well may be the case that the elephant is not sad. It could be the case that what we see as sadness is merely our projection of sadness onto the elephant. Then again, it could very well be that the elephant *is* sad. We seem to think we are the only animals on the planet whose happiness is contingent upon our immediate surroundings. Such thinking is prideful, unsound, and a bit embarrassing. All animals are affected by their environment. If we are going to impose an environment of our own making on other animals, then the very least we can do is take their happiness into consideration.

For elephants who have lived their entire lives in captivity, I can only speculate, with the help of animal behaviorists, anthrozoologists, and ethologists, about their own sense of happiness. Many of the captive elephants in the United States were bred here. It is not as if they have known any other way of life. They have no means of comparing their life of captivity to a life in the wild or a protected park. Nevertheless, there are some telltale signs and other indicators that have to be taken into consideration. As mentioned in chapter 1, their life expectancy in captivity does not present a strong case for continued captivity. The amount of space a captive elephant has is minute to what they seem to require. Add in the claims that these elephants suffer from a host of, arguably, captive-induced problems such as reproductive instability, foot problems, immunodeficiency disorders, various manifestations of psychopathy, and stereotypic behavior that many zoos still refuse to recognize, and captive life for elephants is looking bleak.[6]

6. Tobias, *Behemoth,* 434. Elephant keepers have made a wide and wild variety of claims about why elephants bob and sway their heads. Some of their responses are just baffling. Tobias reports that zoo officials have claimed everything from "the elephants are dancing" to the elephants being happy to see their keepers. This stereotypic behavior is not found in elephants in the wild; it is found only in captivity. It is one of the clearest signs of anxiety, stress, and psychological dis-ease. Zoos and circuses must find a way to

Do elephants belong in zoos? Many people, including zoo officials, are emphatically saying no. Elephants are slowly but surely being phased out of many accredited zoos. Several prominent zoos have already closed their elephant exhibits and have sent their elephants to sanctuaries and breeding centers (which may or may not be a better situation).[7] Many more zoos are pledging to follow suit. Yet, we could broaden the question and ask, does *any* animal belong in a zoo? That is a difficult question to ask, because *belong* is such a loaded term. Do we mean it in the legal sense or do we mean it in the sense of something that is fitting? It is odd enough that humans can claim legal ownership over animals (for instance, we "own" a dog, cat, gecko, and a horse), but what does it mean to say that these animals *belong* in certain places? Zoos can be, and often are, advantageous places for some animals. Zoos are certainly advantageous for a number of species that can no longer live anywhere else. This does not mean, however, that those animals (even the ones zoos are saving) belong there. To say that animals do not belong in zoos is not a condemnation of zoos. We can say the same thing about sanctuaries. It may be the case that elephants do not belong anywhere in Europe or North America.[8] They no more *belong* in wonderful sanctuaries in Tennessee than they belong in zoos filled with wonderful caregivers.[9] I think many people whose lives are dedicated to working in these places agree that elephants do not necessarily belong there. But it is simply naïve to demand that zoos empty their paddocks and send the elephants back to Africa or Asia. Not only would this be a death sentence for many of these animals, elephants in Zimbabwe and Kenya are often considered to be pests. Due

---

appropriately address this behavior if they are going to be able to defend their reasons for keeping them. On a related note, this is also being recognized in orcas. While various sides argue their case for why orcas should or should not be in captivity, no one can easily dismiss the captive orcas' collapsed dorsal fins and the reduction of their life spans by thirty to fifty years (if not more). As with elephants, however, there is no simple answer in terms of what to do with captive-bred or rescued orcas.

7. Such zoos include Detroit Zoo, San Francisco Zoo, Lincoln Park Zoo, Brookfield Zoo, and the Philadelphia Zoo. On a related note, Ringling Bros. and Barnum & Bailey recently made the decision to retire their elephant acts by the year 2018.

8. The gomphothere, an animal that some biologists argue should belong to the elephant family (though gomphothere fossils are not conspecific with African and Asian elephants), roamed the Americas many millions of years ago. Some recent conservationists have proposed introducing elephants into the Americas for the sake of conservation.

9. This is not a stab at zoos and sanctuaries; in fact, it very well may be a defense of them. After all, many of these animals, through no fault of their own, would have no other place to go. We should be grateful that someone is willing to devote their lives to taking care of them.

to inflated numbers, elephants are destroying their environment in such a way that it makes life for humans, as well as a number of endangered species (the black rhino, for example), almost impossible. This occasionally leads to culling, which, in turn, leads to people and institutions in Europe and North America purchasing young elephants so that they will not be destroyed. The politics and ethics of the supposed necessity of culling aside, we cannot blame elephants for their inflated number in some spaces and their subsequent ability to make life difficult on other species. This is not their fault. The problem is not just that we have destroyed many of their habitats. The problem is not just that we have poached and decimated some elephant populations. The problem is not just that we have culled elephants, leading to many of their young ending up in foreign countries. The problem, it seems, is that we have somehow made the entire world inhospitable for elephants. The even bigger problem is that we are making the entire world inhospitable for all animals—including us.

The Pardon of God

Every act of kindness or empathy is always a sort of defiance against the way of the world.

—MATTHEW SCULLY, DOMINION

In his book *Dominion*, Matthew Scully references the wildly impractical and rebellious nature of caring for animals in a world that views them as nothing more than commodified automatons.[10] In a culture in which our treatment of animals tends to benefit us rather than the animals themselves, to do anything for them—to extend grace, mercy, and leniency to those animals forgotten, neglected, and ignored—is an act of rebellion against the pervasively hostile and apathetic spirit that rules our age. In order to counter this spirit, Scully argues, we need more than just laws that protect animals; we need individuals willing to rebel against the assumed practicalities of our time. We need individuals who are unwilling to accept "the way the world is." Just as St. Francis was referred to as a walking "pardon of God" (he always pleaded the case of powerless animals to the powerful and the mighty), we need to become a people who reject the supposed

10. Scully, *Dominion*, 394–98.

practicality and neglectful ease that comes with our one-sided relationships with animals.

We are a species among other species. We live in a world in which it is no longer clear where any of us belong. We are also a species that is in a constant relationship with other species. These relationships are unavoidable. But this does not have to be a bad thing. Relationships between species are what make life possible. From the parasites living in the fur of sloths to insects being excreted out of rabbits, our relationship with other animals must be symbiotic. For those of us who maintain certain convictions about the purpose of life, those relationships must be charitable. Our relationships must nourish rather than oppress. That is the one thing we can do for any animal, whether that animal is indigenous to our region or not. Animals can be cared for and they can be protected. Whether or not captive animals provide us the opportunities to do such things will, probably, be case by case dependent. Conservation centers and zoos certainly have the potential to offer homes for animals who otherwise would not have a home. This does not mean that those animals belong there, but there they are, in our midst, dependent upon us to make their lives a little better. That is a lot to ask of us, but if we are, as so many people pridefully assume, the dominant and governing species, then why can't we do it? If we are as superior as we imagine ourselves to be, then perhaps we can do something worthy of that title. Such a task is beyond the capabilities of zoos, sanctuaries, and conservation centers. It will require a much larger base of people making the changes necessary to enable captive and non-captive animals to flourish. That is not something that should wholly fall on the shoulders of zoos, conservation agencies, and sanctuaries. There is no single entity to blame or to look to for help. Each one of us can make decisions every day that may make this world a little better for others. That responsibility falls to all of us. To paraphrase a popular saying by Jane Goodall, it is not a question of whether we are going to make a difference in the lives of animals—that we already do. The question is, what *kind* of difference are we going to make in their lives?

For an elephant like Hanno, whose circumstances led her from India to Portugal and, finally, to her death in Rome, we can only lament that she was regarded as little more than a gift, a token given by one powerful person to another. Power has shifted, however, and we now find ourselves in positions in which we can improve the lives of countless animals. The circumstances that lead lions to Baghdad, lemurs to North Carolina, and elephants to southeastern Virginia are overwhelmingly convoluted and, sometimes, just plain odd. Some of the situations are good, some of the situations are bad, and some of them are entirely mystifying. Regardless of the where and the how, we have it within our power to make the world a more hospitable home for all animals. I imagine this will require a lot of people committed to a lot of small acts of countercultural generosity. I imagine it will require a lot of people willing to adopt the kind of defiant and rebellious lifestyle that will enable us to become walking pardons of God.

Bibliography

Abram, David. *The Spell of the Sensuous*. New York: Vintage, 1997.

Agamben, Giorgio. *The Open: Man and Animal*. Translated by Kevin Attell. Stanford: Stanford University Press, 2004.

Anthony, Lawrence, with Graham Spence. *Babylon's Ark: The Incredible Wartime Rescue of the Baghdad Zoo*. New York: St. Martin's, 2007.

Atkisson, Sharyl. "Are There Animal Care Problems at National Zoo?" *CBSNews. com*, December 10, 2013. http://www.cbsnews.com/news/are-there-animal-care-problems-at-national-zoo/.

Augustine. *Concerning the City of God against the Pagans*. Translated by Henry Bettenson. New York: Penguin, 1984.

Bahnson, Fred, and Norman Wirzba. *Making Peace with the Land: God's Call to Reconcile with Creation*. Downers Grove, IL: InterVarsity, 2012.

Baur, Gene. *Farm Sanctuary: Changing Hearts and Minds about Animals and Food*. New York: Touchstone, 2008.

Bedini, Silvio A. *The Pope's Elephant: An Elephant's Journey from Deep in India to the Heart of Rome*. New York: Penguin, 1997.

Bekoff, Marc. "Endangered Przewalski's Horse Breaks Neck, Just as National Zoo Releases Neglect Report." *LiveScience.com*, December 13, 2013. http://www.livescience. com/41929-national-zoo-horse-breaks-neck.html.

———. *Ignoring Nature No More: The Case for Compassionate Conservation*. Chicago: University of Chicago Press, 2013.

———. *Why Dogs Hump and Bees Get Depressed: The Fascinating Science of Animal Intelligence, Emotions, Friendship, and Conservation*. Novato, CA: New World Library, 2013.

Berry, Wendell. *Life Is a Miracle: An Essay against Modern Superstition*. New York: Counterpoint, 2001.

———. *The Long-Legged House*. Berkeley, CA: Counterpoint, 2012.

Beston, Henry. *The Outermost House*. New York: Holt, 2003.

Bradshaw, Corey J. A., et al. "Dangers of Sensationalizing Conservation Biology." *Conservation Biology* 21 (2007) 570–71.

Brant, George. *Elephant's Graveyard*. New York: Samuel French, 2010.

Bright, Michael. *The Frog with Self-Cleaning Feet*. New York: Skyhorse, 2013.

Coats, C. David. *Old MacDonald's Factory Farm: The Myth of the Traditional Farm and the Shocking Truth about Animal Suffering in Today's Agribusiness*. New York: Continuum, 1989.

Corwin, Jeff. *100 Heartbeats: The Race to Save Earth's Most Endangered Species*. New York: Rodale, 2009.

Croke, Vicki. *The Modern Ark: The Story of Zoos; Past, Present and Future*. New York: Scribner, 1997.

Davis, Janet. *The Circus Age: Culture and Society under the American Big Top*. Chapel Hill: University of North Carolina Press, 2002.

Darwin, Charles. *The Origin of Species by Means of Natural Selection*. New York: Barnes & Noble, 2004.

Dawkins, Richard. *A Devil's Chaplain: Reflections on Hope, Lies, Science, and Love*. Edited by Latha Menon. New York: Mariner, 2004.

DeStefano, Stephen. *Coyote at the Kitchen Door: Living with Wildlife in Suburbia*. Cambridge: Harvard University Press, 2011.

Dinzelbacher, Peter. "Animal Trials: A Multidisciplinary Approach." *Journal of Interdisciplinary History* 32 (2002) 405–21.

Fialla, Nathan. "How Meat Contributes to Global Warming." *Scientific American* 330 (2009) 72–75.

Finelli, Danielle. "Meat Is Murder on the Environment." *The New Scientist*, July 18, 2007, 15.

Foer, Jonathan Safran. *Eating Animals*. New York: Little, Brown, 2009.

French, Thomas. *Zoo Story: Life in the Garden of Captives*. New York: Hyperion, 2010.

Goodall, Jane, and Marc Bekoff. *The Ten Trusts: What We Must Do to Care for the Animals We Love*. New York: HarperCollins, 2002.

Goodall, Jane, with Phillip Berman. *Reason for Hope: A Spiritual Journey*. New York: Warner, 2003.

Goodall, Jane, with Thane Maynard and Gail Hudson. *Hope for Animals and Their World: How Endagered Speces Are Being Rescued from the Brink*. New York: Grand Central, 2009.

Goudarzi, Sara. "Shark 'Virgin Birth' Confirmed." *National Geographic*, October 10, 2008. http://news.nationalgeographic.com/news/2008/10/081010-shark-virgin-birth-2.html.

Gruen, Lori. *Ethics and Animals: An Introduction*. Cambridge: Cambridge University Press, 2011.

Hancocks, David. *A Different Nature: The Paradoxical Word of Zoos and Their Uncertain Future*. Berkeley: University of California Press, 2001.

Hanson, Elizabeth. *Animal Attractions: Nature on Display in American Zoos*. Princeton: Princeton University Press, 2002.

Hauerwas, Stanley, and John Berkman. "A Trinitarian Theology of the 'Chief End' of 'All Flesh.'" In *Good News for Animals? Christian Approaches to Animal Well-Being*, edited by Charles Pinches and Jay McDaniel, 62–74. Maryknoll, NY: Orbis, 1993.

Hediger, Heini. *Wild Animals in Captivity: An Outline of the Biology of Zoological Gardens*. Translated by G. Sircom. Toronto: General Publishing Company, 1964.

Herzog, Hal. *Some We Love, Some We Hate, Some We Eat: Why It's So Hard to Think Straight about Animals*. New York: HarperPerennial, 2010.

Hribal, Jason. *Fear of the Animal Planet: The Hidden History of Animal Resistance*. Petrolia, CA: CounterPunch and AK Press, 2010.

Hoage, R. J., ed. *Animal Extinctions: What Everyone Should Know.* Washington, DC: Smithsonian Institution, 1987.

Hobgood-Oster, Laura. *The Friends We Keep: Unleashing Christianity's Compassion for Animals.* Waco: Baylor University Press, 2010.

Jamieson, Dale. *Morality's Progress: Essays on Humans, Other Animals, and the Rest of Nature.* Oxford: Oxford University Press, 2002.

Kundera, Milan. *The Unbearable Lightness of Being.* Translated by Michael Henry Heim. New York: Harper, 2009.

Lawrence, Chris. "Report Shows Animal Care 'Severely Lacking' at Smithsonian National Zoo." *CNN*.com, December 13, 2013. http://politicalticker.blogs.cnn.com/2013/12/13/report-shows-animal-care-severely-lacking-at-smithsonian-national-zoo/comment-page-1/.

Leibniz, Gottfried Wilhelm. *Theodicy.* Translated by E. M. Huggard. Edited by Austin Farrer. New York. Cosimo Classics, 2010.

Linzey, Andrew. *Animal Theology.* Urbana: University of Illinois Press, 1995.

MacIntyre, Alasdair. *After Virtue.* 2nd ed. Notre Dame: University of Notre Dame Press, 1984.

Mackay, Richard. *The Atlas of Endangered Species.* New York: Earthscan, 2013.

Martel, Yann. *Beatrice and Virgil: A Novel.* New York: Spiegel & Grau, 2011.

———. *Life of Pi: A Novel.* New York: Harcourt, 2001.

Masson, Jeffrey Moussaieff. *The Face on Your Plate: The Truth about Food.* New York: Norton, 2009.

Masson, Jeffrey Moussaieff, and Susan McCarthy. *When Elephants Weep: The Emotional Lives of Animals.* New York: Delacorte, 1995.

McClendon, James William. *Systematic Theology.* Vol.1, *Ethics.* Nashville: Abingdon, 1986.

Midgley, Mary. *Animals and Why They Matter.* Athens: University of Georgia Press, 1998.

Milbank, John. *Being Reconciled: Ontology and Pardon.* London: Routledge, 2011.

Mullan, Bob, and Garry Marvin. *Zoo Culture.* London: Butler & Tanner, 1987.

Norton, Bryan, et al., eds. *Ethics on the Ark: Zoos, Animal Welfare, and Wildlife Conservation.* Washington, DC: Smithsonian Institution, 1995.

Osborn, Ronald E. *Death Before the Fall: Biblical Literalism and the Problem of Animal Suffering.* Downers Grove, IL: InterVarsity, 2014.

Paquette, S. R. "Importance of the 'Crocodile Hunter' Phenomenon." *Conservation Biology* 21 (2007) 6.

Pimentel, David, and Marcia Pimentel. "Sustainability of Meat-Based and Plant-Based Diets and the Environment." *The American Journal of Clinical Nutrition* 78 (2003) 660S–63S.

Peterson, Dale. *The Moral Lives of Animals.* New York: Bloomsbury, 2011.

Pinches, Charles, and Jay McDaniel, eds. *Good News for Animals? Christian Approaches to Animal Well-Being.* Maryknoll, NY: Orbis, 1993.

Price, Charles Edwin. *The Day They Hung the Elephant.* Johnson City, TN: Overmountain, 1992.

Rowlands, Mark. *The Philosopher and the Wolf: Lessons from the Wild on Love, Death, and Happiness.* New York: Pegasus, 2010.

Saki (H. H. Munro). *The Complete Saki.* New York: Penguin, 1982.

Sartore, Joel. *Rare: Portraits of America's Endangered Species.* Washington, DC: National Geographic, 2010.

Scully, Matthew. *Dominion: The Power of Man, the Suffering of Animals, and the Call of Mercy*. New York: St. Martin's, 2002.

Singer, Peter. *Animal Liberation: A New Ethics for Our Treatment of Animals*. New York: Avon, 1975.

Thomas, of Celano. *St. Francis of Assisi: First and Second Life of St. Francis with Selections from* Treatise on the Miracles of Blessed Francis. Translated by Placid Hermann. Quincy, IL: Franciscan Herald, 1988.

Tobias, Ronald. *Behemoth: The History of the Elephant in America*. New York: Harper Perrennial, 2013.

Vaughan, Brian K. *Pride of Baghdad*. New York: DC Comics, 2006.

Waal, Frans B. M. de. *The Age of Empathy: Nature's Lessons for a Kinder Society*. New York: Harmony, 2009.

Waddell, Helen, trans. *Beasts and Saints*. Grand Rapids: Eerdmans, 1996.

Webb, Stephen. *Good Eating*. Grand Rapids: Brazos, 2001.

———. *On God and Dogs*. Oxford: Oxford University Press, 1998.

Weise, Robert, and Kevin Willis. "Calculation of Longevity and Life Expectancy in Captive Elephants." *Zoo Biology* 23 (2004) 365–73.

Wemmer, Christen M., ed. *The Ark Evolving: Zoos and Aquariums in Transition*. Fort Royal, VA: Smithsonian Institution, 1995.

Wilson, E. O. *The Creation: An Appeal to Save Life on Earth*. New York: Norton, 2007.

———. *The Future of Life*. New York: Knopf, 2002.

York, Tripp. *Third Way Allegiance: Christian Witness in the Shadow of Religious Empire*. Telford, PA: Cascadia, 2011.

York, Tripp, and Andy-Alexis Baker, eds. *A Faith Embracing All Creatures: Addressing Commonly Asked Questions about Christian Care for Animals*. Eugene, OR: Cascade, 2012.

———. *A Faith Encompassing All Creation: Addressing Commonly Asked Questions about Christian Care for the Environment*. Eugene, OR: Cascade, 2014.

About the Author

Tripp York, PhD, teaches in the Religious Studies Department at Virginia Wesleyan College and in the Philosophy and Religion Department at Old Dominion University, both in Norfolk, Virginia. He is the author or editor of a dozen books, including *The Devil Wears Nada*, *Third Way Allegiance*, and the three volume series, *The Peaceable Kingdom*. When he is not teaching or writing, he spends as much time as he can surfing Lake Atlantic.